SHARE A PRAYER TODAY

Ministries

Chronical of Answered Prayer

LANCE FREEZE

BALBOA.
PRESS

A DIVISION OF HAY HOUSE

Balboa Press books may be ordered through booksellers or by contacting:

Balboa Press
A Division of Hay House
1663 Liberty Drive
Bloomington, IN 47403
www.balboapress.com
1-(877) 407-4847

Because of the dynamic nature of the Internet, any web addresses or links contained in this book may have changed since publication and may no longer be valid. The views expressed in this work are solely those of the author and do not necessarily reflect the views of the publisher, and the publisher hereby disclaims any responsibility for them.

The author of this book does not dispense medical advice or prescribe the use of any technique as a form of treatment for physical, emotional, or medical problems without the advice of a physician, either directly or indirectly. The intent of the author is only to offer information of a general nature to help you in your quest for emotional and spiritual well-being. In the event you use any of the information in this book for yourself, which is your constitutional right, the author and the publisher assume no responsibility for your actions.

Any people depicted in stock imagery provided by Thinkstock are models, and such images are being used for illustrative purposes only. Certain stock imagery © Thinkstock.

All scripture quotations, unless otherwise indicated, are taken from the Holy Bible, New International Version®, NIV®. Copyright ©1973, 1978, 1984, 2011 by Biblica, Inc.™ Used by permission of Zondervan. All rights reserved worldwide. www.zondervan.com The "NIV" and "New International Version" are trademarks registered in the United States Patent and Trademark Office by Biblica, Inc.™. All rights reserved.

Printed in the United States of America.

ISBN: 978-1-4525-7181-2 (sc)
ISBN: 978-1-4525-7182-9 (e)

Balboa Press rev. date: 06/07/2013

Table of Contents

Forward

WHEN I BEGAN WRITING THIS book I had no idea that it would become a book. It started out as a blog, simply to attract someone to come into agreement with me in prayer. I heard from some of my favorite Christian teachers that when two or more believers come into agreement about anything according to God's will, then it would be done for them. And I discovered that it works! When I began to see my prayers being answered in a timely manner, I got so excited I had to tell everyone I knew. And most of the people in my circle of friends are not even believers so you can imagine what they were thinking. But the facts still remain. It works for me and I will continue to praise God for answered prayer. I just need to be careful what I ask for and make sure I ask in more detail because God is a God of details. Just look at how wonderfully we are made, in His image.

Prayer is a very powerful and mysterious process suggested by our Creator God as a way for us to communicate with Him, to ask for things, to thank Him for our blessings, to intercede for others and our loved ones, and to simply fellowship with Him. Not all prayers are answered because some prayer is not according to His will and purpose. Find out what is His will and pray for that to be done and it will be done. His will is outlined in His Word. Simply put, whatever is good and in line with Kingdom Principles and the things we might find in His kingdom, such as joy, peace, love, freedom, abundance, prosperity, goodness and things such as these. Aren't these things what we all desire anyway?

For believers, prayer is a very large part of our walk with God. If not, it should be if we want to experience all the wonderful things and feelings our Creator has in store for us. This book is a testimony of my experience with prayer and how God answered so many of mine, despite my sinful nature and short comings and weaknesses. So don't let those things hold you back. The closer one gets to God, the less power these things will have over us. For the most part, prayer is not an instantaneous solution to our problems, rather it is a process. Start today!

From family restoration to financial breakthroughs and the wonderful freedom I enjoy today. God has been faithful to me when I pray according to His will for me. So my advice to everyone is get as much of the 'Word' in you as possible, come to Him with a sincere heart and don't let your sins and short comings hold you back from getting closer to your Creator, He loves you just the way you are, more than you will ever know and He's just waiting for you to come to Him so He can show you.

May God bless you with many answered prayers and the blessed assurance of everlasting life in heaven with Him. Praise His name!

As this is my first attempt at self- publishing, the reader may find some minor mistakes in grammar, spelling, and punctuation. Please bare with me in this and understand that I am a new author with many things to learn and understand. In spite of these minor errors, I pray that the prayers recorded in these pages will become the prayers of the reader and will come into agreement with many and experience the same blessings and answered prayers that I have now and in the future. Volume 2 of "Share a Prayer Today" is in the final stage of completion and will be published soon with less mistakes and even more interesting content. May the God of heaven bless you with all good things and many answered prayers of your own. In the name of Jesus, Yeshua, our Lord and King, make it so...

Dedications

I AM DEDICATING THIS BOOK first to the Lord God Yahweh, Jesus the Christ, and the Holy Spirit by which we receive the power to do these things. And to my family and friends who support and encourage me to study and gain knowledge so I can share with them the awesome power of prayer and what is has done in my life and also in the lives many others who embrace it.

Dad and Moms- Lance, Dorothy, Donna, and Marlis

X-Wives- Becky, Debbie

My children and grandchildren- David, Shawna, Deinara, Cassie, and Ryan

Brothers and Sisters- Teresa, Lancette, Angie, John, Annette, Nelson, Rob and Sheree

Friends-Rick, Doc, Joe, Dan D., Becky, George, Terry, Jeri, Sandi, Mandy, Troy and Andrea, Ricky, Bill, Ben ,Tristan, and my very special and newest friend and blessing, Cleta, who's invalueable help, support, and encouragement , helped to make this dream come true and prayer to be answered.

And my teachers- Joyce Myer, John Hagee, Pat Robertson, Joseph Prince, Creflo Dollar, Rabbi Jonathan Bernis, Andrew Womac, Gary Kessee, Rabbi Kirt Schneider May God Bless all the people who have made a profound impact on my life. I pray for them the same things I pray for myself, Joy, Peace, Love, Divine Creativity and Discernment, Freedom, Abundance, and Prosperity. May the blessings of God chase after them and saturate them with all good things. Let them all be blessed to be a blessing. In the name of Jesus, Yeshua, Make it so…

JANUARY 2011

Monday, January 17, 2011

DAILY SHARE A PRAYER TODAY

Lord God, Thank You for today and all the blessings You've given me today. I thank You that I am a blessing to my family and friends. That I am learning how to use the gifts You've given me and I am moving into abundance and prosperity. I thank You that You are teaching me great and mighty things that I do not know. I accept all that You have for me and will find it joyful to share with others as You Lead me. Thank You Lord. In Jesus name, make it so.

Posted by lance at

PRAYER TO SHARE

Lord God,
From the light of God that I am,
From the love of God that I am,
From the power of God that I am,
From the heart of God that I am.

I decree:
I dwell in the midst of infinite abundance. The abundance of God is my infinite source.
The river of life never stops flowing. It flows through me into lavish expression.
Good comes to me through unexpected avenues and God works in a myriad of ways to bless me.
I now open my mind to receive my good. Nothing is too good to be true. Nothing is too wonderful to have happen. With God as my source nothing amazes me.

I am not burdened by past or future. One is gone the other is yet to come.

By the power of my belief, coupled with my purposeful , fearless actions and my deep rapport with God my future is created and my abundance is made manifest.

I ask and I accept that I am lifted in this and every moment into higher truth. My mind is quiet.

From this day forward I give freely and fearlessly into life and life gives back to me with magnificent increase. Blessings come in expected and unexpected ways. God provides for me in wondrous ways. I am indeed grateful and I let it be so. AMEN

This prayer was shared with me by Simona Rich, a friend on face book and You tube. This young lady is totally inspiring and wise beyond her years.

Posted by lance at 6:53 AM

Tuesday, January 18, 2011

WHAT IS FAITH

What is faith? It is the confident assurance that what we hope for is going to happen. It is the evidence of things we cannot yet see. Hebrews 11:1 NLT

Posted by lance at 9:23 AM

Wednesday, January 19, 2011

WISDOM SCRIPTURE

James 1-5 says, "If anyone of you is deficient in wisdom, let him ask of the giving God [who gives] to everyone liberally and ungrudgingly, without reproaching or faultfinding and it will be given him."

Posted by lance at 12:38 PM

PRAYER FOR TODAY

Lord God, I thank You for another day and a chance to be closer to You. Lord I ask for wisdom and courage as I make the most of this day. Help me to know Your will for me and let me share Your word with all who will listen. I know that Your Word is the source of life and Your promises will be kept. Thank You for being my God and Father. In Jesus name, make it so.

Posted by lance at 8:11 AM

ENCOURAGING WORDS FROM "THE WORD"

And we can be confident that He will listen to us whenever we ask Him for anything in line with His will. And if we know He is listening when we make our requests, we can be sure He will give us what we ask for. 1 John 5:14-15

Posted by lance at 8:03 AM

Thursday, January 20, 2011

THE PRAYER OF FAITH JAMES 5:13-16

"Is any one of you in trouble? He should pray. Is anyone happy? Let him sing songs of praise. Is any one of you sick? He should call the elders of the church to pray over him and anoint him with oil in the name of the Lord. And the prayer offered in faith will make the sick person well; the Lord will raise him up. If he has sinned he will be forgiven. Therefore confess your sins to each other and pray for each other so that you may be healed. The prayer of a righteous man is powerful and effective." James 5:13-16

Posted by lance at 7:45 PM

SMOKERS PRAYER

Heavenly Father, Thank You for blessing me with a healthy body. Lord I'm asking for Your help with my addiction to tobacco. Please take the desire away from me to smoke. Smoking really stinks and I know You would pleased if I quit. I need Your help with this Lord. By the power of the Holy Spirit, according to Your Word, In the name of Jesus, make it so, Amen

Posted by lance at 1:34 PM

SPECIAL PRAYER

Father God, Please bless and heal Paige Who has H1N1 and is in the hospital. We lift her up to You Lord and we ask that she be healed in Jesus name, by the power of the Holy Spirit, according to Your Word, make it So, Amen

Posted by lance at 11:11 AM

5

PRAYER FOR TODAY

Lord God, Thank you for Your Word and the wisdom that it teaches. Thank You also for all those who are led to share Your Word with others. Lord, help me to be a better giver today. Help me have the faith to be obedient and not only hear Your Word but to do it also. Father, I pray now for healing of a person who is dear to me who has breast cancer. Heal her now Lord! By the power of the Holy Spirit remove the cancer from her body in the name of Jesus! Thank You Jesus for answering this prayer. Amen

Posted by lance at 7:45 AM

WISDOM SCRIPTURE FOR TODAY

Luke 6:38 says "Give and it will be given to you. A good measure, pressed down, shaken together and running over, will be poured into your lap. For with the measure you use, it will be measured to you."

Posted by lance at 7:30 AM

Saturday, January 22, 2011

SCRIPTURE FOR TODAY

Elijah was a man just like us. He prayed earnestly that it would not rain, and it did not rain on the land for 3 and 1/2 years. Again he prayed and the heavens gave rain, and the earth produced its crops. Luke 5:17-18

Posted by lance at 4:31 PM No comments

Sunday, January 23, 2011

PRAYER TO SHARE

Lord God Almighty, Thank You for being my God and creator. Thank You for your mercy and grace. Thank You for blessing me despite my sinful nature. Your Word is our guide and I thank You for those that teach Your Word and for the Holy Spirit that lets us understand it. Father according to Your Word help me to become a better person, a blessing to many, a light in the darkness. Let Your Holy Spirit inspire me and bring glory and honor to your name. Thank You for love, joy, peace, kindness, mildness, faithfulness, patience, self control and goodness. According to Your Word, make it so, Amen.

Posted by lance at 8:06 AM

MARK 4:26-27

He also said, "This is what the kingdom of God is like. A man scatters seed on the ground. Night and day whether he sleeps or gets up the seed grows, though he does not know how."

Posted by lance at 7:52 AM

Monday, January 24, 2011

MORE ABOUT ME.

Hi visitors and fellow believers, peace be with you. Shalom

I believe in prayer and what it can do. God has answered so many of my prayers I am convinced that I have His favor. For whatever reason, I don't have a clue. I just know I'm led to share my prayers. If anyone will believe with me in agreement then these things will eventually happen. For example; I prayed to be closer to my daughter and her mom. Long story short, they now share half my house. That would not have been possible just three years ago but it has come manifest in the last year. That one prayer, at the time I prayed it was crazy, it was just something I knew was impossible but I always prayed about it any way. God did it!!! Things just happened!!! God is so real and good! Even my property was an answer to a prayer. I simply prayed for a nice house with a pond and some woods. Within 5 years I ended up with a small cottage and two rental mobile homes on 23 acres, more than 1/2 woods, nice trees and a large in pond in front. I only wish I'd gone into more detail when describing what I ask God for. I recommend when you pray with me add details and even write it down on paper and carry it around with you. I've written prayers in a note book and just leave it lying around where I can see it. I just know in faith believing God will give me what I ask for as long as it is something good and in His will.

I'm excited about this blog because I know it will help someone get their prayers answered and their faith strengthened and maybe even lead to getting some one saved!!! Wow! Glory to God!!! Praise His Name!!! These prayers I've been sharing have come from my heart except when I come across one that really got my attention. But most will be things I want to happen in my own life. I believe there are many people who want the same basic things I want but just don't know how to ask God for it. Or just need someone to come into agreement with. I've learned that it's important to find someone to be in agreement with you because it seems to make things happen sooner. That's why I started this blog not only to help others but for me too. You can actually help my prayers to come true just by closing your eyes and agreeing with me in faith that God hears us and will bless us for having faith that He is "the rewarder of those that diligently seek Him."

Tell your friends to visit and pray with me also. The more the better!!!

The stronger we'll all be!! Thanks for being here and can't wait to hear comments and prayers being answered GOD BLESS ALL OF YA.

Posted by lance at 2:19 PM

SCRIPTURE FOR TODAY PROVERBS 15:8

The LORD detests the sacrifice of the wicked, but the prayer of the upright pleases Him.

Posted by lance at 8:52 AM

PRAYER FOR TODAY FOR FAMILY

Heavenly Father, In Jesus name I thank You for all my blessings. For my children and grandchildren. Bless them Lord, with good health and joy and peace and prosperity and abundance and especially a place in Your kingdom. Father, help me to be a great blessing to them. Help me to teach them Your Word by example and help me to provide for them richly. Bless their mother with good health and joy and security Lord help her to want to know You better and save her a place in Your kingdom. Watch over all the rest of my friends and family and keep them safe in these last days and help me to be a blessing to them also. I pray for the peace of Jerusalem and protection for your people around the world. In Jesus Name, by the power of the Holy Spirit, make it so Amen.

Posted by lance at 8:49 AM

Tuesday, January 25, 2011

PRAYER FOR TODAY

LORD, I thank you for all my blessings. All the good in my life and I ask for more good things to happen. I know You want me to be joyful and happy and healthy and You are showing me how by the power of the Holy Spirit and Your Word. Lord, I want to be free of financial bondage and lack so that I can be a better and bigger giver and bring more glory and honor to Your name. So I can be a greater blessing to my family and friends and even to those that don't know me. I want to be a testimony to Your power when we come to You In faith believing. You are a good God and I know You Love me and want me to share Your word with others. Thank You for answering my prayers Lord, in Jesus name by the power of the Holy Spirit, according to Your Word , make it so, amen

Posted by lance at 9:12 AM

WISDOM SCRIPTURE

Commit to the LORD whatever you do, and your plans will succeed. Proverbs 16:3

Posted by lance at 8:56 AM

Wednesday, January 26, 2011

PRAYER FOR BLESSINGS

LORD God, Thank you for this day and another chance to receive the good You have in store for me. I know You are a good God, the only true God ,and You are my father, my creator. Father, I receive the blessings You have for me today and I give You thanks! I bring glory and honor to your name as I share Your Word and will with others. And I show my gratitude by my obedience the best I can. I grow stronger every day as my faith grows. Thank You Lord, in Jesus name, by the power of the Holy Spirit, according to Your Word Amen.

Posted by lance at 4:39 PM

SCRIPTURE FOR BLESSING NUMBERS 6:24-26

"'THE LORD BLESS YOU AND KEEP YOU;
THE LORD MAKE HIS FACE SHINE UPON YOU
AND BE GRACIOUS TO YOU;
THE LORD TURN HIS FACE TOWARD YOU
AND GIVE YOU PEACE."

Posted by lance at 4:17 PM

Friday, January 28, 2011

WHAT SALVATION MEANS

IN THE OLD TESTAMENT TIMES God required from his people a sacrifice, a blood sacrifice, to pay for or atone for the sins of His people, the Israelites or Jews. Usually the sacrifice was a ram, goat, sheep or bull, spotless and without blemish, brought to the alter and killed as a holy sacrifice. This was required regularly at the temple in Jerusalem.

AS THE PROPHETS FORETOLD ABOUT the chosen one, Jesus, would be sent by God the Father as ransom sacrifice for the sins of the world. "For God so loved the world that He gave his one and only son, that whoever believes in Him shall not perish but have everlasting life. For God did not send His son into the world to condemn the world, but to save the world through Him." John 3:16-17

JESUS WAS "THE LAMB OF God that takes away the sins of the world". Because Jesus was "spotless" and "without blemish" or sinless He was the only acceptable sacrifice for that purpose. He , Jesus is the Jewish Messiah and the savior of all those who trust God and put their faith in Him. That is the good news, or "Gospel" that we as Christians believe and are commissioned to spread all over the earth as a testimony to Gods truth and Word. If you believe that Jesus died for your sins and was resurrected say the following prayer out loud and accept Jesus today. He really does love us and wants us with Him in His kingdom.

Posted by lance at 8:05 PM

SALVATION PRAYER

Lord God, I believe You sent your son Jesus down here to die as a sacrifice for my sins and the sins of the world. And I believe that He, Jesus, rose from the dead on the third day and is at Your right hand in heaven. I accept You, Jesus, as my Lord and Savior. I confess with my mouth and believe in my heart that You are Lord. Thank You Jesus, I am Saved!

Posted by lance at 7:35 PM

PRAYER TO SHARE TODAY

Lord God, Thank You again for another day of blessings, a day of life that You have made, let me experience joy today and receive all the good things You have in store for me. Thank You Father for answering my prayers. Peace in Jerusalem and protection for your people in Jesus name, by the power of the Holy Spirit, according to your Word, Amen

Posted by lance at 8:59 AM

SCRIPTURE FOR TODAY MATTHEW 7:7-8

Ask and it will be given to you; seek and you will find; knock and the door will be open for you. For everyone who asks receives; he who seeks finds; and to him who knocks the door will be open.

Posted by lance at 8:53 AM No

Saturday, January 29, 2011

ALTERNATIVES???

THOUGHT FOR TODAY

What are the alternatives of not accepting Jesus as Lord? Eternal separation from the light of God, an existence of distress and fear, pain and suffering in darkness forever.

If you believe you do not have a creator and that there is no "God", what then is the purpose of your life? What do you have to look forward to when your years here on this earth are spent? What if there really is a God in heaven who loves you and only wants you to accept Him as your creator and will reward you with eternal life and you refuse Him? Think about this. It really is a no brainer to be a believer and accept the free gift of God which is eternal life in place of indescribable beauty and peace. I choose to believe I have a creator who loves me and wants me to be with Him forever in paradise. It's a choice we all will have to make some day. Choose life!

Posted by lance at 7:57 AM

PROTECTION PRAYER

Lord God, Today I ask You to protect my family and all my friends and loved ones from the coming hardships that will happen according to your Word. Father I pray that those who have not accepted You yet will come to know You by the power of the Holy Spirit and be saved. Help me Father to share what I know with them and help them to understand how much You want them to accept You as Lord and Savior. How simple You have made it for them to come to You and be saved. Thank You Lord. In Jesus name by the power of the Holy Ghost according to Your Word, Amen.

Posted by lance at 7:39 AM

MAY GOD BLESS ALL OUR PRAYER PARTNERS

Lord God of Heaven and Earth, May You richly bless all our prayer partners in all that we do. By the power of the Holy Spirit in Jesus name, Amen.

Posted by lance at 2:46 PM

PRAYER FOR SELF CONTROL

Lord God, Thank You for today and a chance to serve You and be a blessing to someone. Father, I ask that Your Word be strong in me today and help me to resist the temptation that might come on me. By the power of Your Spirit help me to turn from the things I know that displease You and let me be in Your favor today and be a testimony to Your grace. Let the fruit of the Spirit, self control, be strong in me today and every day. Help me to be a good influence on someone and be an encourager to someone today. I especially need to control my tongue, Lord, sometimes I say things that I wish I wouldn't say, please help me to choose my words wisely and bring glory and honor to Your name. Thank You for hearing my prayer, in the name of Jesus, by the power of the Holy Spirit, according to your word, Amen

Posted by lance at 9:00 AM

WHAT IS REPENTANCE?

THOUGHT FOR TODAY

A lot of believers think that repentance means being Holy "perfect" and not sinning. Being like a monk or a catholic nun. That idea turns many would be believers against the true gospel message which is salvation by Gods grace, His undeserved kindness towards us. In reality, we are all born in sin and we will never be free of it until we die and go to heaven.

However, we can be free of the "guilt" associated with sin if we accept the free gift of God, salvation by the blood of our Lord Jesus, who died for the sins of the world. That is GOOD NEWS! That is THE GOSPEL Message. John the Baptist message was "Repent! and be baptized and God will forgive your sins". In the Greek repent meant to change our way of thinking about the things we did that displeased God and then we would be gradually free from the wrong doing. I don't think any of us can be perfect on earth but we can change our way of thinking by the power of the Holy Spirit, there by changing our habits. If we were all sinless we wouldn't need a savior. Repent from wrong thinking and everything else will take care of itself. Then we will have the peace of mind the Lord promised us and be free from the "guilt" of sin. "The truth will set us free".

Posted by lance at 8:42 AM

Monday, January 31, 2011

PRAYER FOR TODAY PREPARATION FOR HARD TIMES TO COME

Heavenly Father, Let all the believers take notice of the warning signs and prepare for the hard times to come. As we watch Your prophesy's unfold before our eyes help us get ready and not fear the coming destruction. Let us have the faith we need to be in Your favor and come through it all and into Your kingdom. It's what we all look forward to, Lord. Having a place prepared for us in Your kingdom. Help us to be a blessing to those that are yet unsaved and to guide them to You Lord, by the power of the Holy Spirit according to Your Word, in Jesus mighty name, Amen

Posted by lance at 9:07 AM

SCRIPTURE FOR TODAY GALATIANS 5:22-23

"But the fruit of the spirit is love, joy, peace, patience, kindness, goodness, faithfulness, gentleness and self-control. Against such things there is no law."

Posted by lance at 8:54 AM No

15

FEBRUARY 2011

Tuesday, February 1, 2011

PRAYER FOR TODAY PREPARATION FOR HARD TIMES TO COME

Lord God, please help me to be prepared for the hard times to come. As we watch Your prophesies coming true before our eyes let us not be afraid and know that You will protect us and guide us in the way we should go. Help me to be a blessing to those who don't know You and lead as many as I can to You to be saved from the coming destruction. Thank You Lord, for hearing my prayers and for loving me. Help me to do Your will and not be afraid. In Jesus name, by the power of the Holy Spirit, according to Your Word, Amen.

Posted by lance at 8:11 AM

SCRIPTURE FOR TODAY MATTHEW 12:8-10

"I tell you, whoever acknowledges me before men, the Son of Man will also acknowledge him before the angels of God. But he who disowns me before men will be disowned before the angels of God. And everyone who speaks a word against the Son of Man will be forgiven, but anyone who blasphemes against the Holy Spirit will not be forgiven".

Posted by lance at 8:02 AM

Wednesday, February 2, 2011

WISDOM SCRIPTURE FOR TODAY PROVERBS 1:7

"The fear of the LORD is the beginning of knowledge, but fools despise wisdom and discipline."

Posted by lance at 2:21 PM

PRAYER FOR ACCEPTANCE

Lord God, Thank You for all my blessings, and thank You for Your undeserved kindness which is a free gift. I receive it now ,Lord even though nothing I can do will be enough for me to earn it. I thank You for Your mercy and grace that saved me from eternal darkness and separation from Your love. Guide me, and direct me now Father and show me what I should do to bring glory and honor to Your name that I might find favor in Your eyes to show my gratitude for You. Thank You. In Jesus name, by the power of the Holy Spirit, according to Your Word, Amen.

Posted by lance at 11:13 AM

SCRIPTURE FOR TODAY EPHESIANS 2:8-10

"For it is by grace you have been saved, through faith - and this not from yourselves, it is the gift of God - not by works, so that no one can boast. For we are God's workmanship, created in Christ Jesus to do good works, which God prepared in advance for us to do".

Posted by lance at 11:01 AM No comments:

Thursday, February 3, 2011

PRAYER FOR CONFESSION OF SINS

Lord God of Heaven, I confess all the wrong things I've done in the past and all the things I may do in the future. I know I am a sinner Lord and I need Your mercy and grace for my salvation. I know I was born in sin and that Jesus came to deliver me from all unrighteousness. Thank You, Lord, for forgiving me and setting me free from the guilt of sin. Help me to not do the things I know to be wrong. You know me Lord, You know my weaknesses and my strengths. Help me to be strong and resist the temptations that stumble me. Thank You Lord, for forgiving me, In Jesus name, By the power of the Holy Ghost, make it so, amen.

Posted by lance at 7:54 AM

SCRIPTURE FOR TODAY 1JOHN1:9

"If we confess our sins, He is faithful and just and will forgive our sins and purify us from all unrighteousness".

Posted by lance at 7:43 AM

Friday, February 4, 2011

SPECIAL PRAYER FOR HEALING AND RECOVERY

Lord God of heaven, Thank You for hearing our prayers and blessing us with your underserved kindness. Lord, today I ask that You help the mother of a friend to recover quickly and fully from the surgery she will undergo today. We lift her up to You now Lord and ask that you remove all fear and uncertainty from her heart and mind and that she be made whole and happy and full of joy. We ask that You bring her closer to You and let her feel Your love and healing power. Thank You Lord, In Jesus name, by the power of the Holy Spirit, according to your word, Amen.

Posted by lance at 7:02 AM

SCRIPTURE FOR TODAY JOHN 5:24

"I tell you the truth, whoever hears my word and believes Him who sent me has eternal life and will not be condemned; he has crossed over from death to life".

Posted by lance at 6:46 AM

Saturday, February 5, 2011

SCRIPTURE FOR TODAY 1 JOHN 5:13-15

"I write these things to you who believe in the name of the Son of God so that you may know that you have eternal life. This is the confidence we have in approaching God; that if we ask anything according to His will, He hears us. And if we know that He hears us---whatever we ask---we know that we have what we ask of Him".

Posted by lance at 4:13 AM

PRAYER FOR APPROACHING GOD

Lord God, You are my creator. You made me in Your image according to Your Word. I believe what You say in Your word is true. Now I come to You in prayer knowing that You hear me and that You love me and only want the best for me as a father wants for his children. Thank You Lord God for loving me and caring for me. My requests are simple and are in line with Your Word and I know that You will consider what I ask for in Jesus name according to Your word. Lord, what I want is wisdom, joy, peace of mind, forgiveness, love, freedom from lack, prosperity, and health to enjoy the life You've given me. Power to overcome addiction, and the opportunity to help others know You, and especially a place in Your kingdom. Thank You for hearing my prayer and being my God and Father in Jesus name, according to your Word ,Amen.

Posted by lance at 4:05 AM

Sunday, February 6, 2011

SCRIPTURE FOR TODAY 1 JOHN 4:16-17

"And so we know and rely on the love God has for us." "God is love. Whoever lives in love lives in God, and God in him. In this way love is made complete among us so that we will have confidence on the Day of Judgment, because in this world we are like Him."

Posted by lance at 7:44 AM

PRAYER FOR LOVE

Lord God, You are love, help me to be more loving to the people around me and even to people I don't know. Please put it in my spirit to have the kind of love that it takes to help others know You. To be a better example of what a true follower of Jesus is. To show the world that You are a God of love and grace. Put it in my spirit to love others the same way you love us and in return I will be loved by others. Thank You Lord, in Jesus name, by the power of the Holy Spirit, according to Your Word, Amen

Posted by lance at 7:36 AM

Monday, February 7, 2011

PRAYER FOR PROSPERITY AND ABUNDANCE.

Heavenly Father, I know You only want the best for me and my family and I thank You now for all the good in my life, my children and grandchildren, the friends I have, the house I live in, food and hot running water to name just a few. Lord, help me to have more than enough so I can be a blessing to others. Let me know abundance and prosperity beyond my greatest expectations. Let me know freedom from lack and worry and good health to enjoy this life You've given me. Thank You Lord. In Jesus name, by the power of the Holy Ghost, according to Your word, Amen.

Posted by lance at 4:42 AM

SCRIPTURE FOR TODAY NUMBERS 6:24-26

"The LORD bless you and keep you; the LORD make His face shine upon you and be gracious to you; the LORD turn His face toward you and give you peace."

Posted by lance at 4:32 AM

Tuesday, February 8, 2011

SCRIPTURE FOR TODAY PSALM 103:8-12

"The LORD is compassionate and gracious; slow to anger, and abounding in love. He will not always accuse nor will He harbor His anger forever; He does not treat us as our sins deserve or repay us according to our iniquities. For as high as the heavens are above the earth so great is His love for those who fear Him; as far as the east is from the west, so far has He moved our transgressions from us".

Posted by lance at 4:42 AM

PRAYER FOR GUIDANCE

Good morning Lord! Thank You for this Day and all my blessings. Father, today I ask for guidance and direction as I go through this day. Help me to think good thoughts, positive thoughts, and help me to be encouraging to others around me. Help me to think like You think and act as You would act according to Your Word. In Jesus name, by the power of the Holy Ghost, Amen.

Posted by lance at 4:34 AM

Wednesday, February 9, 2011

SCRIPTURE FOR TODAY JEREMIAH 29:11-13

"For I know the plans I have for you declares the LORD, plans to prosper you and not to harm you, plans to give you hope and a future. Then you will call upon Me and come and pray to Me, and I will listen to you. You will seek Me and find Me when you seek Me with all your heart".

Posted by lance at 4:44 AM

PRATER FOR TODAY

LORD, I just want to tell You thanks again for all my blessings. Thank You for my job, for the house we live in, for good food, for love and joy, for my friends and family, for my children and grandchildren, for Your Word which is true and wise, and above all, for the hope of everlasting life with You. Thank You LORD, in Jesus name, by the power of the Holy Spirit, Amen.

Posted by lance at 4:38 AM

Thursday, February 10, 2011

PRAYER FOR TODAY

Lord God , Today I ask You to give me courage to share the Good News with others as You would see fit. That I might be an instrument of Your will to people who need to hear the Gospel message. Help me to be bold and confident and accurate in what I say. Thank You Lord, In Jesus name, Amen

Posted by lance at 4:51 AM

SCRIPTURE FOR TODAY EPHESIANS 1:9

"And He made known to us the mystery of his will according to his good pleasure, which He purposed in Christ, to be put into effect when times have reached their fulfillment-- to bring all things in heaven and on earth together under one head, even Christ".

Posted by lance at 4:47 AM

Friday, February 11, 2011

MESSAGE TO PRAYER PARTNERS

My Blog Is here for people to get closer to the God who created them by way of His Word and other believers coming together in agreement in prayer. To talk to God and ask Him for the things that

are according to His Word. Healing, Wisdom, Joy, Prosperity, Love, and all the fruits of Gods Holy Spirit! It's all for the asking!! But only to those who believe. "Ask and you shall receive"!!" Do YOU receive it today!!!! The God of heaven loves you!!!! Return it by believing Him and having "faith" in Him.

Posted by lance at 8:37 PM

MARK 10:13-16

"People were bringing little children to Jesus to have Him touch them, but the disciples rebuked them. When Jesus saw this He was indignant. He said to them," Let the little children come to me, and do not hinder them, for the kingdom of God belongs to such as these, I tell you the truth, anyone who will not receive the kingdom of God like a little child will never enter it". And He took the children in His arms, put His hands on them and blessed them".

Posted by lance at 4:57 AM

PRAYER FOR PATIENCE AND TOLERANCE FOR OTHERS

Lord God, Thank You for Your Word that teaches us Your mind and the way You think. Without Your word as a guide we'd all be lost. Thank You for being merciful and understanding toward us especially in these last days when there are so many false prophets and teachers out there to confuse us and mislead us. Give us the same patience and tolerance You have for us, who stumble, to show to others who are trying to serve You the best they can. Help us to be more like You Lord. Thank You for hearing this prayer in Jesus name, according to Your Word, Amen.

Posted by lance at 4:49 AM

Saturday, February 12, 2011

SCRIPTURE FOR TODAY MATTHEW 11:28-30

"Come to me, all you who are weary and burdened, and I will give you rest. Take my yoke upon you and learn from me, for I am gentle and humble in heart, and you will find rest for your souls. For my yoke is easy and my burden is light".

Posted by lance at 4:55 AM

PRAYER FOR REST

Lord God, I thank You for all my blessings, I know I can't thank You enough for what You have done for me and will do in my future. You are the Most High God, creator of heaven and earth and You love me and care for me. I'm sorry that I am a sinner Lord help me to make better choices in things I do and say. I need rest Lord in my heart, mind, and body. I want to serve You Lord, let me know how and give me the courage and the strength to do Your will. In Jesus name, By the power of the Holy Ghost, Amen.

Posted by lance at 4:48 AM

Sunday, February 13, 2011

PROVERBS 16:24

"Pleasant words are a honeycomb, sweet to the soul and healing to the bones".

Posted by lance at 8:24 AM

PRAYER FOR TODAY SELF CONTROL

Lord God, Today I ask again that You help me with self control. I know self control is one of the fruits of the Holy Spirit and probably the hardest one to practice, at least for me. Today let me think about what I say before I say it, and what I do before I do it and then choose to do what is good in Your sight and say what is right. I ask forgiveness for the times when I make mistakes and do and say things I know aren't right. Thank You Lord for helping me and forgiving me. Thank You for Your mercy and undeserved kindness. In Jesus name, By the power of the Holy Spirit, according to Your Word, make it so, Amen.

Posted by lance at 8:20 AM

Monday, February 14, 2011

SCRIPTURE FOR TODAY ISAIAH 1:18-19

"Come now, let us reason together" says the LORD. "Though your sins are like scarlet, they shall be white as snow; though they are red as crimson, they shall be like wool."

Posted by lance at 4:52 AM

PRAYER TO HELP OTHERS KNOW GOD

Lord God, Help me today not to feel guilty about the blessings I have when I see others around me less fortunate and living in fear and insecurity. Help me to share with them the wisdom and knowledge that can only be found in your Word. Help me to guide them to You that as many as have the heart to know You will be saved and have a more abundant life as they will learn how to serve You in action and words. In Jesus name, by the power of the Holy Spirit, according to Your Word, Amen.

Posted by lance at 4:45 AM

Tuesday, February 15, 2011

SCRIPTURE FOR TODAY JAMES 5:14-15

"Is anyone of you sick? He should call the elders of the church to pray over him and anoint him with oil in the name of the Lord. And the prayer offered in faith will make the sick person well; the Lord will raise him up. If he has sinned, he will be forgiven".

Posted by lance at 4:54 AM

PRAYER FOR HEALING

Lord God, You are the "Great Physician" according to Your word and I believe Your Word. I believe all things are possible with You and through You. Today I prayer for my grandson Ryan, Lord, that You will take away whatever it is that's making him sick. Doctor says he may have asthma. Lord heal him now in Jesus name, by the power of the Holy Spirit. Thank You Lord, Thank You. We lift him up to You now in prayer believing You will make him healthy and whole and protect him from all forms of illness and accidents in Jesus name, Amen.

Posted by lance at 4:49 AM

Wednesday, February 16, 2011

SCRIPTURE FOR TODAY PROVERBS 11:25

"A generous man will prosper; he who refreshes others will himself be refreshed".

Posted by lance at 4:48 AM

PRAYER TO BE GENEROUS

Lord, help me to have faith in Your Word and be generous to others whenever I can. Help me to be a cheerful giver. Bless me Lord with abundance so I can be a blessing to others and bring glory and honor to your name. Thank You Lord for giving me wisdom. In Jesus name, make it so, Amen.

Posted by lance at 4:46 AM

Thursday, February 17, 2011

SCRIPTURE FOR TODAY PROVERBS 3:13-14

" Blessed is the man who finds wisdom, the man who gains understanding, for she is more profitable than silver and yields better returns than gold. She is more precious than rubies, nothing you desire can compare with her".

Posted by lance at 4:49 AM

SPECIAL THANKS

Thank You God for healing my grandson of his sickness. My faith be in You always, Amen.

Posted by lance at 4:45 AM

PRAYER FOR WISDOM

Lord God Of Heaven and Earth, Lord , please help me to understand Your Word because I know all wisdom comes from it. Help me to share it with others and draw them to You according to Your will and purpose. Thank You Lord for answering my prayers. Thank You for Your mercy and grace. In the name of Jesus, by the power of the Holy Spirit, Amen.

Posted by lance at 4:43 AM

Friday, February 18, 2011

SCRIPTURE FOR TODAY MALACHI 3:10-11

"Bring the whole tithe into the store house, that there might be food in my house. "Test me in this says the LORD ALMIGHTY, " and see if I will not throw open the flood gates of heaven and pour out a blessing that you will not have room enough for it". I will prevent pests from devouring your crops, and the vines in your fields will not cast their fruit," says the LORD ALMIGHTY".

Posted by lance at 4:58 AM

PRAYER TO BELIEVE GOD

Lord God , Help me to take to heart the things I learn from Your word. Help me to have faith in what You say and know that You only want the best for me. I know that You are God and I need to be obedient and do what You say because it will only help me in this life. Thank You for Your Word and the wisdom that it teaches. In Jesus name, by the power of the Holy Spirit, Amen.

Posted by lance at 4:48 AM

Saturday, February 19, 2011

SCRIPTURE FOR TODAY LUKE 12:22-23

"Then Jesus said to His disciples:" Therefore I tell you, do not worry about your life, what you will eat; or about your body, what you will wear. Life is more than food, and the body more than clothes".

Posted by lance at 5:03 AM

PRAYER OF JESUS

Read JOHN 17:20-26 Jesus prays for all believers.

Posted by lance at 4:52 AM

Sunday, February 20, 2011

SCRIPTURE FOR TODAY PROVERBS 15:16

"Better a little with the fear of the LORD
than great wealth with turmoil."

Posted by lance at 8:27 AM

SONG LYRICS I WROTE BASED ON PSALM 40

I was waiting for the LORD,
Then He heard my cry
He lifted me up and wiped the tears from my eyes

He put a new song in my heart
and peace in my mind
A song of praise to Him who made the earth moon and sky

He told me that He loved me
more than I could know
And if I'd only trust Him then I'd never be alone

Blessed is the one that makes the LORD his trust
Many Oh LORD are the wonders You have done < CHORUS>
So I will not seal my lips our salvation it has come
Through Jesus Christ our Savior the Spirit of Your Son
The blessing of His blood.

He put a new song in my heart
And peace in my mind
I'll praise Him to the people I'll praise Him till I die
Posted by lance at 8:24 AM

Monday, February 21, 2011

SCRIPTURE FOR TODAY MARK 16:15-16

He said to them "Go into all the world and preach the good news to all creation.

Whoever believes and is baptized will be saved, but whoever does not believe will be condemned".

Posted by lance at 5:08 AM

SONG LYRICS TO "THANK YOU LORD JESUS"

Here's another song I wrote to bring glory and honor to God and Our Lord Jesus. I sing it all the time, in the truck, in the shower, even at work when I can. I believe the Lord likes it.

Thank You Lord Jesus, for all my blessings,
Thank You Lord Jesus for watching over me,
Thank You Holy Spirit for all my wisdom
Thank You Holy Spirit for guiding me.

When the Holy Spirit shines His light on you
There isn't no telling what the Lord will do,
He can heal the sick and make a blind man see <CHORUS
Oh Lord, have mercy on me
I thank You Lord Jesus
For watching over me.

Your Word is revelation for all creation
Your Word is revelation for us to see
When the Holy Spirit shines His light on you
There isn't no telling what the Lord will do

He can heal the sick and make a blind man see
Oh Lord set the prisoners free

Thank You Lord Jesus for all my blessings
Thank You Lord Jesus for watching over me
When the Holy Spirit shines His light on you
There isn't no telling what the Lord can do
He can heal the sick and make a blind man see
He can lift a poor man out of poverty

Thank You Lord Jesus for all my blessings
Thank You Lord Jesus for watching over me.
Lance Freeze.

Posted by lance at 5:03 AM

Tuesday, February 22, 2011

SCRIPTURE FOR TODAY MATTHEW 5:43-46

"You have heard that it was said, "Love your neighbor and hate your enemy" But I tell you: Love your enemies and pray for those who persecute you, that you may be sons of your Father in heaven. He causes the sun to rise on the evil and the good, and sends rain on the righteous and the unrighteous. If you love those who love you, what reward will you get? Are not even the tax collectors doing that"?

Posted by lance at 4:24 PM

PRAYER FOR ENEMIES

Lord God, Help me to forgive those who do not understand me and who would destroy me. Let me help them come to know You and be saved. My desire is to serve You, Lord and You have said, "Love your enemies".

I understand what You mean. Make peace and do good to them that they may feel Your Spirit and turn from the evil thoughts they might have against me. Help me to lead them to You by my words and deeds. Thank You for this wisdom. Help me to practice this daily and watch my enemies turn into brothers and sisters in You. In Jesus name, by the power of the Holy Spirit, Amen.

Posted by lance at 4:14 PM

Wednesday, February 23, 2011

2 PETER 1:12-14

"So I will always remind you of these things, even though you know them and are firmly established in the truth you now have. I think it is right to refresh your memory as long as I live in the tent of this body, because I know that I will soon put it aside, as our Lord Jesus Christ has made clear to me".

Posted by lance at 4:47 AM

PRAYER FOR STRONGER FAITH

Lord God of the Bible, Thank You Lord for being my God and my hope. I love You Lord and I love Your Word. You are the one and only God, creator of heaven and earth. Lord help my faith in You to grow and become more powerful to be a testimony to Your love and grace. I know I am a sinner and I need Your mercy and grace for my salvation. Help me to do what Your word says and not just hear it but to practice it. And let all those around me see that Your Word is real and wonderful and that it has awesome power. To heal and to comfort and to provide for all our needs. Thank You Lord, in Jesus name, by the power of the Holy Ghost, Amen.

Posted by lance at 4:34 AM

Thursday, February 24, 2011

1 JOHN 2: 1-2

"My dear children, I write this to you so that you will not sin. But if anybody does sin, we have one who speaks to the Father in our defense-- Jesus Christ the Righteous One. He is the atoning sacrifice for our sins, and not only for ours but also for the sins of the whole world".

Posted by lance at 5:00 AM

PRAYER TO NOT SIN

Heavenly Father, Help me to be more righteous and good. I know I'm a sinner, and I thank You for accepting me the way I am and molding me into what I can be. Thank You for loving me despite My sinful nature. I really want to be pleasing to You, Lord. Help me to be a better person and be in Your favor and bless me Lord with all the blessings You promise us. Thank You for sending Your one and only Son as a perfect sacrifice to atone for all our sin. In Jesus name, by the power of the Holy Spirit, according to Your Word, Amen.

Posted by lance at 4:54 AM

Friday, February 25, 2011

SCRIPTURE FOR TODAY 1 JOHN 3:16-18

"This is how we know what love is: Jesus Christ laid down His life for us. And we ought to lay down our lives for our brothers. If anyone has material possessions and sees his brother in need but has no pity on him, how can the love of God be in him? Dear children, let us not love with words or tongue but with actions in truth".

Posted by lance at 4:19 AM

PRAYER TO SHOW LOVE

Lord God, Thank You Abba Father, for loving me unconditionally. Help me to do likewise to my neighbors and those I come in contact with. Help me to share my love with others who may not know You and by doing so bring glory and honor to your name and fulfill what is written: "Love your neighbor as yourself." Help me to renew my mind with thoughts of love and compassion rather than revenge and resentment. Help me to do good to my enemies, those who wish to bring me down. I forgive all who wrong me and wish them peace and prosperity and a place in Your kingdom. In Jesus name, make it so, Amen.

Posted by lance at 4:11 AM

Saturday, February 26, 2011

SCRIPTURE FOR TODAY PSALM 35:4-6

"May those who seek my life be disgraced and put to shame;
may those who plot my ruin be turned back in dismay.
May they be like chaff before the wind,
with the Angel of the LORD driving them away;
may their path be dark and slippery,
with the angel of the LORD pursuing them".

Posted by lance at 10:45 AM

PRAYER FOR PROTECTION FROM ENEMIES

Lord God of heaven, Thank You Lord for protecting me from those who seek to hurt and destroy me. You know the ones I'm talking about. Lord I forgive them for the lies and deceit; I forgive them for their evil intentions toward me. I'm asking You Lord according to Your word to protect me and keep me from harm and ruin and damaged relationships. Lord I pray in Jesus name according to Your word, and by the power of the Holy Spirit, make it so, Amen.

Posted by lance at 10:37 AM

Sunday, February 27, 2011

SCRIPTURE FOR TODAY MATTHEW 6:14-15

"For if you forgive men when they sin against you, your heavenly Father will also forgive you. But if you do not forgive men their sins, your Father will not forgive your sins".

Posted by lance at 8:24 AM

PRAYER TO FORGIVE ENEMIES

Lord God, Help me to forgive those who mean to cause me harm for no other reason but jealousy and envy. I ask that You send an angel and deal with them. Not to hurt them, but to turn their attention away from me and my loved ones. I wish for them peace and joy and all the things I would have for myself and mine. I just want freedom from the harassment and threats. I forgive them, Lord. But I don't have to be friendly with them, do I? In Jesus name, by the power of the Holy Ghost, Amen

Posted by lance at 8:16 AM

Monday, February 28, 2011

SCRIPTURE FOR TODAY HEBREWS 10:25

"Let us not give up meeting together, as some are in the habit of doing, but let us encourage one and other-- and all the more as you see the Day approaching".

Posted by lance at 4:41 AM

PRAYER FOR PREPARATION

Lord God, In Jesus name help me prepare for the hard times to come. The times that You have warned us would come upon the world. Help me with resources enough to support my entire family and all my friends. Even strangers that may need help. Help me with wisdom and knowledge and courage to get through these terrible times until You come and rescue all of us who have Faith in You and Your promises. Thank You Lord for Your love and protection, in Jesus name, by the power of the Holy Spirit, Make it so, Amen.

Posted by lance at 4:38 AM

MARCH 2011

Tuesday, March 1, 2011

SCRIPTURE FOR TODAY ISAIAH 40:29-31

"He gives strength to the weary and increases the power of the weak. Even youths grow tired and weary, and young men stumble and fall; but those who hope in the LORD will renew their strength. They will soar on wings like eagles; they will run and not grow weary, they will walk and not be faint".

Posted by lance at 4:50 AM

PRAYER FOR STRENGTH

Lord God, Give me strength in these last days to help my family and loved ones get through the hard times to come. Help me be confident and positive about all things. Let my resources increase so I will have more to give and direct me where I should help. I love You Lord and I love Your Word, You are an awesome Father and I thank You for being my God. In Jesus name, by the power of the Holy Spirit, Amen.

Posted by lance at 4:45 AM

Wednesday, March 2, 2011

HEBREWS 11:6

"And without faith it is impossible to please God, because anyone who comes to Him must believe that He exists and that He rewards those who earnestly seek Him".

Posted by lance at 4:47 AM

PRAYER TO BE PLEASING TO GOD

Heavenly Father, I pray that You help me to be pleasing to You by the things I say and do. Help me to be a doer of Your word and not just a hearer. Help me to know what You want from me and to be obedient to Your will. I'm sorry when I do things that aren't right and good in Your eyes. Please help me to have right thoughts and live a clean and moral life. Thank You Lord, In Jesus name, according to Your Word, Amen

Posted by lance at 4:44 AM

Thursday, March 3, 2011

SCRIPTURE FOR TODAY LUKE 4:40-41

"When the sun was setting, the people brought to Jesus all who had various kinds of sickness, and laying His hands on each one, He healed them. Moreover, demons came out of many people, shouting, "You are the son of God!" But He rebuked them and would not allow them to speak, because they knew He was the Christ".

Posted by lance at 6:23 AM

PRAYER FOR HEALTH

Lord God of Heaven, Thank You for a healthy body and mind. Let us be healed of any infirmity by the power of the Holy Spirit according to Your Word. We can serve You best when we are healthy and happy knowing you are our "great physician". You are our healer and our provider when we have faith believing. Thank You Lord, for all our blessings. You are God and there is no other, I love You lord and I love Your Word. Your Word is wisdom and power. Thank You Lord, in Jesus name by the power of the Holy Ghost, Amen.

Posted by lance at 6:12 AM

Friday, March 4, 2011

SCRIPTURE FOR TODAY PHILIPPIANS 4:6-7

"Do not be anxious about anything, but in everything, by prayer and petition, with thanks giving, present your request to God. And the peace of God, which transcends all understanding, will guard your hearts and minds in Christ Jesus".

Posted by lance at 4:57 AM

PRAYER FOR PATIENCE WHILE WAITING ON GOD

Lord God, Help me to have patience while I wait on You to answer prayer. Time does not exist with You as it does for me. I know You hear my prayers and will answer in Your own time. Help me to ask for things according to Your will and purpose because You are good all the time and Your ways are right and just. When I pray for others to be healed please help them as soon as possible to bring glory and honor to Your name and let them know beyond doubt that You are real and You love them, thank You Lord for answering my prayers in Jesus name, by the power of the Holy Ghost, according to Your Word, make it so, Amen.

Posted by lance at 4:51 AM

Saturday, March 5, 2011

SCRIPTURE FOR TODAY PHILIPPIANS 4:8-9

"Finally brothers, whatever is true, whatever is noble, whatever is right, whatever is pure, whatever is lovely, whatever is admirable--- if anything is excellent or praiseworthy---- think about such things. Whatever you have learned or received or heard from me--- put it into practice. And the God of peace will be with you".

Posted by lance at 4:51 AM

PRAYER FOR RIGHT THOUGHTS

Lord God, Please help me to renew my mind and think about the good things around me. Help me to think positive thoughts even if the people around me and the circumstances may not be so positive. Help me to create a positive atmosphere around me by the things I say, do, and think. I know that this will bring glory and honor to Your name because those around me will sense Your presence, the fruits of Your spirit are love, joy, peace, kindness, mildness, faithfulness, patience, self control and goodness. Let these things be in me and let me share these things with others. In Jesus name, by the power of the Holy Spirit, Amen.

Posted by lance at 4:44 AM

Sunday, March 6, 2011

SCRIPTURE FOR TODAY ROMANS 8:1-4

"Therefore, there is now no condemnation for those who are in Christ Jesus, because through Christ Jesus the law of the Spirit of life set me free from the law of sin and death. For what the law was powerless to do in that it was weakened by the sinful nature, God did by sending His own Son in the likeness of sinful man to be a sin offering. And so He condemned sin in sinful man, in order that the righteous requirements of the law might be fully met in us, who do not live according to the sinful nature but according to the Spirit".

Posted by lance at 8:21 AM

PRAYER OF THANKS FOR FORGIVENESS OF SINS

Lord God, I thank You Lord for forgiveness of all my sin, past, present and future. Thank You for loving me enough to send Your one and only son to die as a sacrifice for the sins of the world. I know I can do nothing to deserve what You did for me, but I can try to serve You the best I can to show my love and appreciation for what You did for me. I can give You my time, I can be as obedient to Your Word as I can, I can share my resources with others and I can share my knowledge and wisdom with anyone who will listen. Thank You Lord for Your undeserved kindness which is Your Grace and mercy. In Jesus name, by the power of the Holy Spirit, Amen.

Posted by lance at 8:10 AM

Monday, March 7, 2011

SCRIPTURE FOR TODAY MATTHEW 12:36-37

""But I tell you that men will have to give account on the day of judgment for every careless word they have spoken. For by your words you will be acquitted, and by your words you will be condemned".

Posted by lance at 4:48 AM

PRAYER FOR CONTROLLING MY TONGUE

Lord God in Jesus name I ask that You help me control what I talk about and what I say. I tend to want to tell stupid jokes that could be offensive to some and I tend to use bad language when I'm at work and around some of my friends. Every time I talk bad I think about how that reflects on what I truly believe in my heart and how You must be disappointed in what You hear. I ask forgiveness for the things I say and help from Holy Spirit in controlling my tongue to bring glory and honor to Your name, and set an example for others to follow. Thank You for forgiving me and being my Lord and God, In Jesus name, by the power of the Holy Ghost, Amen

Posted by lance at 4:44 AM

Tuesday, March 8, 2011

SCRIPTURE FOR TODAY NUMBERS 6:24-26

"The LORD bless you and keep you; the LORD make His face shine upon you and be gracious to you; the LORD turn His face toward you and give you peace."

Posted by lance at 4:54 AM

PRAYER FOR BLESSINGS

Lord God, Today I thank You again for all my blessings and ask You to bless me with a greater understanding of Your Word so I can share with others and draw them closer to You. I still struggle with self control where my tongue is concerned. It seems like I say things before I have a chance to think about what I sound like. Help me Lord , I know I won't be able to change without Your help. I need You to zap me with Your Spirit and change the things I say before I say them. Sometimes I can't believe the things that come out of my mouth, as a believer I am ashamed of myself. I just have a hard time controlling what I say. Please Help. In Jesus name, by the power of the Holy Spirit, Amen.

Posted by lance at 4:49 AM

Wednesday, March 9, 2011

MESSAGE TO NEW PARTNERS AND VISITORS

Thank you all for your interest in Share A Prayer Today. We pray that this blog will be a great blessing to you and that you will see your prayers answered and get closer to God in these last days. May the Lord Jesus be with you and give you peace and may the wisdom of God be in you and help you in this life, in Jesus name, by the power of the Holy Spirit , Amen

Posted by lance at 7:56 PM

SCRIPTURE FOR TODAY LUKE 18:15-17

"People were bringing babies to Jesus to have Him touch them. When the disciples saw this, they rebuked them. But Jesus called the children to Him and said, "Let the little children come to me and do not hinder them, for the kingdom of God belongs to such as these. I tell you the truth, anyone who does not receive the kingdom of God like a little child will never enter it".

Posted by lance at 5:13 AM

PRAYER FOR CHILDREN AND GRANDCHILDREN

Lord God, In Jesus name I ask that You draw my children and grandchildren closer to You and let them feel Your love and mercy and let them know the peace and joy that comes with serving You. Lord, I pray that You will keep them safe and happy in these last days and help them to have good lives here on earth till Your kingdom comes. Let them have a desire to serve You and the ability to understand Your word. Help me to be a good example for them to follow let me share my knowledge and wisdom with them. Thank You Lord, in Jesus name by the power of the Holy Spirit, Amen.

Posted by lance at 5:06 AM

Thursday, March 10, 2011

SPECIAL PRAYER FOR HEALING AND RECOVERY

Lord God, In the name of Jesus we ask that You have mercy on a man with cancer. Tom Vincent J. is in need of immediate healing Lord. He is a believer and needs a healing miracle Lord, we lift him up to You and pray in Jesus name that You Heal him and show Your mighty power according to Your Word, In Jesus name, Amen

Posted by lance at 7:17 PM

SPECIAL PRAYER FOR PACY M.

Lord God, in the mighty name of Jesus Christ we lift up little 3 month old Pacy M. to You Lord. This child of yours was diagnosed with pneumonia and needs healing today Lord, Thank You for Your tender mercy and love for little children. In Jesus name, by the power of the Holy Spirit, Amen.

Posted by lance at 7:12 PM

SCRIPTURE FOR TODAY EPHESIANS 6:4

"Fathers, do not exasperate your children; instead, bring them up in the training and instruction of the Lord".

Posted by lance at 4:50 AM

PRAYER FOR CHILDREN AND GRANDCHILDREN

Lord God, I pray that You will protect my children and grandchildren from all forms of illness and accidents. Guard their minds from wrong thinking and bad influences so that they will have happy and joyful lives and they will know You are God and there is no other. Send angels to guide them and direct them and protect them in these last days. Help me to be a positive influence on them and teach them Your Word and the Good News about what Jesus did for us all. Thank You Lord, In Jesus name by the power of the Holy Ghost, Amen.

Posted by lance at 4:46 AM

Friday, March 11, 2011

SPECIAL FOR TSUNAMI VICTIMS IN JAPAN

Lord God, in Jesus name we pray that those affected by the tsunami in Japan be comforted as they go through this terrible time. Help them to recover mentally, physically, and financially from this disaster and let all those in a position to help do so with a generous and loving heart to bring glory and honor to Your name. And let this be a time to share the gospel message with those who would otherwise not hear it. In Jesus name, by the power of the Holy Ghost, Amen.

Posted by lance at 7:33 PM

SCRIPTURE FOR TODAY MATTHEW 7:7-8

"Ask and it shall be given to you; seek and you will find; knock and the door will be open to you. For everyone who asks receives; he who seeks finds; and to him who knocks, the door will be opened".

Posted by lance at 4:51 AM

PRAYER FOR DIVINE CREATIVITY

Lord God, Thank You for all my blessings and for watching over me and my family. Lord, today I ask for divine creativity and new ideas to better serve You and bring glory and honor to Your name and experience prosperity and abundance beyond what I can ask and hope for. I pray that I can be a blessing to many and have much to share with others including financial resources. Part of Your will is to give generously to those in need and to help widows and fatherless children. Help me to be in a position where I can give more and help more and bring glory to Your name by sharing the gospel with those who may never have heard it. Thank You Lord, in Jesus name, according to Your Word, Amen

Posted by lance at 4:44 AM

Saturday, March 12, 2011

SCRIPTURE FOR TODAY HEBREWS 10:19-23

"Therefore, brothers, since we have the confidence to enter the Most Holy Place by the blood of Jesus, by the new and living way opened for us by the curtain, that is, His body, and since we have a great priest over the house of God, let us draw near to God with a sincere heart in full assurance in faith, having our hearts sprinkled to cleanse us from a guilty conscience and having our bodies washed with pure water. Let us hold unswervingly to the hope we profess, for He who promised is faithful".

Posted by lance at 4:42 AM

PRAYER FOR OVERCOMING ADDICTIONS

Lord God, in Jesus name I thank You today for setting me free from the cigarette habit. I know in my heart I could not have done it without You.

Several of my friends and co workers ask me how I did it and I point to You. How You changed my mind toward tobacco because I ask with a sincere heart. You delivered me from something that was destroying me. I know You can do the same thing with other addictions. Please set me free from the other habits that are destructive and help me to change my mind about the things You have warned us about. Thank You Lord, In Jesus name, Amen

Posted by lance at 4:29 AM

Sunday, March 13, 2011

SPECIAL PRAYER FOR JAPANESE EARTH QUAKE AND TSUNAMI VICTIMS AND SURVIVORS

Lord God, In Jesus name, Have mercy on the many lost souls that perished in Japan due to the disaster that happened on 3-11-11. May You comfort the survivors and heal them physically, mentally, and emotionally from the pain and suffering they must be going through. May You have special mercy for the unsaved and for those who have not heard the Gospel message and prepare a place for them in Your Kingdom. Thank You Lord, for Your mercy, Your Love, and Your grace, in Jesus name, by the power of the Holy Ghost, Amen.

Posted by lance at 7:23 PM

SCRIPTURE FOR TODAY HEBREWS 11:1-3

"Now faith is being sure of what we hope for and certain of what we do not see. This is what the ancients were commended for. By faith we understand that the universe was formed at God's command, so that what is seen was not made out of what is visible".

Posted by lance at 10:43 AM

PRAYER FOR MORE FAITH

Lord God, In Jesus name, I thank You for all my blessings and for being my Lord and savior. I have faith in You Lord. I know that You are real and You live today and that You are at the right hand of the Father God. Also that He Gave You all power and authority in heaven and earth according to Your Word. Lord, I need more faith, stronger faith, proven faith, I just feel like I don't have enough faith even though I believe and I am serving You the best I can. Help me Lord, I don't know exactly how You will help me but I know You will. Thank You. In Jesus name, by the power of the Holy Spirit, according to Your Word, Amen

Posted by lance at 10:37 AM

Monday, March 14, 2011

SCRIPTURE FOR TODAY JOHN : 14:1-4

"Do not let your hearts be troubled. Trust in God; trust also in me. In my Father's house there are many rooms; if it were not so I would have told you. I am going there to prepare a place for you. And if I go and prepare a place for you I will come back and take you to be with me that you also may be where I am. You know the way to the place where I am going".

Posted by lance at 4:37 AM

PRAYER FOR STRENGTH TO RESIST TEMPTATION

Lord God, In Jesus name I pray for the strength to resist the temptations that do harm to me and those I love. Forgive me for my weaknesses and help me to change my mind regarding the things the enemy keeps bringing to my attention. Replace those things with good things that will help me and those I love and even people I don't know. Help me to do Your will Lord, not mine. Help me to have the peace that surpasses all understanding and the joy that comes only when we live according to Your will. Help me to be free from all these temptations the same way You delivered me from my tobacco habit so that I might be a testimony to Your power and mercy and grace. Thank You Lord, in Jesus name, according to Your Word, Make it so, Amen

Posted by lance at 4:29 AM

Tuesday, March 15, 2011

SCRIPTURE FOR TODAY MARK 11:22-26

"Have faith in God," Jesus answered, "I tell you the truth, if anyone says to this mountain, "Go, throw yourself into the sea", and does not doubt in his heart but believes that what he says will happen, it will be done for him. Therefore I tell you, whatever you ask for in prayer, believe that you have received it, and it will be yours. And when you stand praying, if you hold anything against anyone, forgive him, so that your Father in heaven may forgive you your sins".

Posted by lance at 10:57 AM

PRAYER FOR MIRACLES TO HAPPEN

Lord God, in Jesus name I pray for miracles to happen here for me and for miracles to happen everywhere in the world to bring glory and honor to Your name. Healing miracles, family miracles, legal miracles, natural miracles, financial miracles, miracles of every kind, Lord let it be so! Your Word tells us how to make it happen and how to receive miracles from You. Help us to practice Your word and to do Your Word not just to hear it. Give us understanding and discernment and strengthen us in our walk with You Lord. You are the only way to eternal life and pure joy, help us to receive this wisdom and use it to have a more abundant and joyful life and to share with others the things You give us. In Jesus name, make it so, Amen.

Posted by lance at 10:46 AM

Wednesday, March 16, 2011

MATTHEW 6:19-21

"Do not store up for yourselves treasures on earth, where moth and rust destroy, and where thieves break in and steal . But store up for yourselves treasures in heaven, where moth and rust do not destroy, and where thieves do not break in and steal. For where your treasure is, there your heart will be also".

Posted by lance at 5:01 AM

PRAYER FOR AWARENESS

Lord God, in The name of Jesus, I ask that You help me be aware of who I am in You. Help me to know what I can do by the power of the Holy Spirit. I want to bring glory and honor to Your name and hear Your voice say, "Well done good and faithful servant". Let me also be aware of those who speak lies and would draw me away from the truth that sets us free from sin and guilt. Help me to understand Your Word and share it with others and draw people to You according to Your will. Thank You Lord for hearing my prayers and answering them, You are awesome and I love You, Lord and I love Your word. In Jesus name, according to Your Word, Amen.

Posted by lance at 4:54 AM

Thursday, March 17, 2011

SCRIPTURE FOR TODAY 5:14-16

"You are the light of the world. A city on a hill cannot be hidden. Neither do people light a lamp and put it under a bowl. Instead they put it on its stand, and it gives light to everyone in the house. In the same way, let your light shine before men, that they may see your good deeds and praise your Father in heaven."

Posted by lance at 4:55 AM

PRAYER TO HEAR GODS VOICE

Lord God of the Bible, in Jesus name I ask that I can hear Your voice more clearly and know that it is You that is talking to me and not just me thinking. I know that You speak to us in a still, small, voice but sometimes I'm not sure if it's You, or just me talking to myself in thought. When You talk to me, I'd like to hear an audible voice, as if I was talking to a friend. But I know that this a rare occurrence and probably won't happen to me, but if it did, it would be awesome. I guess I just would like to hear from You with words to guide me. I will keep on doing what You want me to do the best way I can. Thank You for using me and for blessing me with certain gifts. In Jesus name, by the power of the Holy Spirit, Amen.

Posted by lance at 4:48 AM

Friday, March 18, 2011

SCRIPTURE FOR TODAY 2 CORINTHIANS 12:9-10

"But he said to me, "My grace is sufficient for you, for my power is made perfect in weakness". Therefore I will boast all the more gladly about my weaknesses, so that Christ's power may rest on me. That is why, for Christ's sake, I delight in weaknesses, in insults, in hardships, in persecutions, in difficulties. For when I am weak, then I am strong."

Posted by lance at 4:56 AM

PRAYER OF THANKS FOR GRACE

Lord God of heaven and earth, thank You Lord for your grace, which is undeserved kindness and love. If not for Your grace none of us would ever see your kingdom or experience the fruits of Your Holy Spirit. All I can say is Thank You, Lord for loving me and blessing me with Your Word. I pray for Your strength when I am weak and Your mercy when I fail. Help me to be a better man, a more obedient man, because You are the only way to everlasting life, and I choose life. Thank You God, Thank You Jesus. In Jesus name, By the power of the Holy Spirit, according to Your Word, Amen.

Posted by lance at 4:47 AM

Saturday, March 19, 2011

SCRIPTURE FOR TODAY EPHESIANS 3:16-19

"I pray that out of his glorious riches he may strengthen you with power through His Spirit in your inner being, so that Christ may dwell in your hearts through faith. And I pray that you, being rooted and established in love, may have power, together with the saints, to grasp how wide and long and high and deep is the love of Christ, and to know this love that surpasses knowledge---that you may be filled to the measure of all the fullness of God."

Posted by lance at 4:57 AM

PRAYER FOR ABUNDANCE AND PROSPERITY

Heavenly Father, Abba, Thank You for all the blessings You have given me and for understanding me and helping me to understand myself. Thanks for giving me a future and a better life here until Your kingdom comes to this world according to Your Word. I know that many of us in this country live far better than most of the world's population. A double wide mobile home on a small plot of land is like a mansion to most people in other countries. A 10.00 dollar an hour job is prosperity to someone in Mexico or China. I just thank You for what I have and ask that You help me to be more creative in ways to increase my resources so I will have more to share. Thank You , in Jesus name, Amen.

Posted by lance at 4:47 AM

Sunday, March 20, 2011

SCRIPTURE FOR TODAY ROMANS 12:1-2

"Therefore I urge you, brothers, in view of God's mercy, to offer your bodies as living sacrifices, holy and pleasing to God---this is your spiritual act of worship. Do not conform any longer to the pattern of this world, but be transformed by the renewing of your mind. Then you will be able to test and approve what God's will is---His good, pleasing and perfect will".

Posted by lance at 9:31 AM

PRAYER FOR RENEWING OF MY MIND

Lord God, In Jesus name thank You for Your word. I know Your word is true and reliable and tells us things we need to know to make our lives better and more joyful. Help me to train my mind to think more like You think and act the way You might act and share my knowledge with all those who want to know. I understand that You want only for us to love You as our Father and creator and to do Your word not just hear it. Help me Lord to be a doer of Your Word. There are so many reasons why I want this I can't tell You in a short prayer. The most important is "wisdom", Help me to renew my mind daily and take in Your wisdom and share it with others. Wisdom is a gift more valuable than money. Thank You Lord for giving us Your wisdom. Help me to receive it today by the renewing of my mind. In Jesus name, according to Your Word, Amen.

Posted by lance at 9:23 AM

Monday, March 21, 2011

SCRIPTURE FOR TODAY JOHN 17:20-

"My prayer is not for them alone. I pray also for those who will believe in me through their message, that all of them may be one, Father, just as You are in me and I am in You. May they also be in us so that the world may believe You have sent me. I have given them the glory that You gave me, that they may be one as we are one: I in them and You in me. May they be brought to complete unity to let the world know that You have sent me and have loved them even as You have loved me."

Posted by lance at 4:59 AM

PRAYER FOR GIVING THANKS

Lord God, In Jesus name I thank You for this day and for all the days to come that they be filled with joy and peace and a spirit of true freedom that only comes with knowing Your truth about the "Good News" of the Gospel message. Thank You Lord for abundance and prosperity and good health. Thank You Lord that I have more than enough so I can give generously to others in need and bring glory and honor to your name. I thank You Lord for all my blessings and pray that You will continue to bless me even more richly as I reach out to You and serve You the best I can. In Jesus name, By the power of the Holy Spirit according to Your Word, Amen.

Posted by lance at 4:49 AM

Tuesday, March 22, 2011

SCRIPTURE FOR TODAY MARK 9:38-41

"Teacher," said John, "we saw a man driving out demons in your name and we told him to stop, because he was not one of us."

"Do not stop him ," Jesus said. "No one who does a miracle in my name can in the next moment say anything bad about me, for whoever is not against us is for us. I tell you the truth, anyone who gives you a cup of water in my name because you belong to Christ will certainly not lose his reward".

Posted by lance at 4:52 AM

PRAYER FOR INCREASE AND ABUNDANCE

Lord God of the Bible, In Jesus name I pray for increase and abundance that brings peace of mind and security. I know it's Your will that Your people live in security and peace as Your sons and daughters. I want to experience that peace and freedom that comes with Your blessings. I ask that You bless me with more prosperity and freedom and peace of mind in these last days and that I am a blessing to my family and friends and even to people I don't know to bring glory and honor to Your name. Thank You Lord, for Your word, and for Your grace and mercy, in Jesus name, by the power of the Holy Spirit, Amen

Posted by lance at 4:43 AM

Wednesday, March 23, 2011

MARK 6:4-6

Jesus said to them, " Only in his home town, among his relatives and in his own house is a prophet without honor." He could not do any miracles there, except lay his hands on a few sick people and heal them. And he was amazed at their lack of faith.

Posted by lance at 4:44 AM

PRAYER FOR THIS DAY

Lord God, I thank You for this day and all my blessings. Thank You for my wonderful kids and grand kids. Thank You for my whole family, for my job and for every good thing in my life. Thank You for Your Word, which is my guide and the Holy Spirit my comforter. Thank You, In Jesus name, by the power of the Holy Ghost, Amen.

Posted by lance at 4:36 AM

Thursday, March 24, 2011

SCRIPTURE FOR TODAY JAMES 1:26-27

"If anyone considers himself religious and yet does not keep a tight rein on his tongue, he deceives himself and his religion is worthless. Religion that God our Father accepts as pure and faultless is this: to look after orphans and widows in their distress and to keep one's self from being polluted by the world".

Posted by lance at 4:50 AM

PRAYER TO CONTROL TONGUE

Lord God, in Jesus name Help me to control my tongue. I still tend to say the wrong things at the wrong times. Not all the time, but enough to where I'm disappointed in myself and embarrassed at times and wonder why I said such stupid and ignorant things. I need special help from You Lord when it comes to controlling my tongue. All I can do now is ask forgiveness and thank You for Your mercy and Your grace. I really need the Holy Spirit to help me out here in whatever way He can. Thank You Lord, in Jesus name by the power of the Holy Spirit, Amen.

Posted by lance at 4:41 AM

Friday, March 25, 2011

SCRIPTURE FOR TODAY 1 PETER 1:3-6

"Praise be to the God and Father of our Lord Jesus Christ! In His great mercy he has given us new birth into a living hope through the resurrection of Jesus Christ from the dead, and into an inheritance that can never perish, spoil, or fade---kept in heaven for you, who through faith are shielded by Gods power until the coming of the salvation that is ready to be revealed in the last time. In this you greatly rejoice, though now for a little while you may suffer grief and all kinds of trials."

Posted by lance at 4:47 AM

SPECIAL MESSAGE TO PARTNERS AND VISITORS

I feel led to start using Gods name and the Hebrew name of our Lord Jesus in my prayers. To me, it just seems like the right thing to do as "God" and "Lord" are really titles and not personal names. I've been thinking about this for quite a while and I believe the Holy Spirit has put this in my heart to do. I would suggest anyone who is skeptical about this do research on the names of God and find out for themselves what I have. God's name, "Yahweh" means "I am who I am" or "I am that I am". In English it is pronounced "Jehovah" Our Lord Jesus name is "Yeshua" in Hebrew. I think using these names will cultivate a more personal relationship with Our Heavenly Father and our Lord Jesus. May God bless us all and give us the desires of our hearts and life everlasting in paradise with Him. In the name of Yeshua, Amen

Posted by lance at 4:34 AM

Sunday, March 27, 2011

SCRIPTURE FOR TODAY 1 PETER 2:1-3

"Therefore rid yourselves of all malice and all deceit, hypocrisy, envy and slander of every kind. Like new born babies, crave pure spiritual milk, so that by it you may grow up in your own salvation, now that you have tasted that the Lord is good".

Posted by lance at 9:19 AM

PRAYER FOR PROVISION

Lord God, Yahweh, creator of heaven and earth. Thank You God for providing for my family and me in these last days. You are "Jehovah Jire", "God my Provider", according to Your Word. I need only to accept Your gifts with faith believing that Your word is true. I receive the abundance of the universe as You freely give to me and I in turn obey Your Word and share with others the provisions You provide. I share wisdom and knowledge with all who will listen and learn as I have. Thank You for protecting us in these last days from all forms of Illness and injury and from any weapon formed against us according to Your Word. Help us to be a doer of Your Word and not just a hearer. In the name Jesus, Yeshua, the Christ, make it so, Amen

Posted by lance at 9:11 AM

Monday, March 28, 2011

SCRIPTURE FOR TODAY PSALM 40:11-12

"Do not withhold your mercy from me, O LORD; may your love and your truth always protect me; for troubles without number surround me; my sins have over taken me, and I cannot see. They are more than the hairs on my head, and my heart fails within me".

Posted by lance at 4:51 AM

PRAYER FOR PROTECTION

Lord God, Yahweh, creator of heaven and earth, thank You for Your mercy and grace. Thank You for the wisdom that is in Your Word. Lord I pray that You protect my family in these last days and lead us on a path to Your kingdom. Forgive us for our sins and help us to serve You the best way we can. Help us to think the way You think and say the things You say and be more like our savior, Jesus. Thank You Father, for hearing this prayer. In the name of Jesus, Yeshua, the Messiah, Amen.

Posted by lance at 4:46 AM

Tuesday, March 29, 2011

SCRIPTURE FOR TODAY PSALM 38:19-22

"Many are those who are my vigorous enemies; those who hate me without reason are numerous. Those who repay my good with evil slander me when I pursue what is good. O LORD, do not forsake me, O my God. Come quickly to help me, O LORD my Savior".

Posted by lance at 4:55 AM

PRAYER FOR ISRAEL

Lord God, Yahweh, I pray for the peace of Jerusalem and peace in Israel and protection for Your people around the world according to Your Word. Lord. I also pray for the enemies of Israel that they may see that hatred of the Jewish people is not the answer to the problems they face. I pray that the enemies of Israel may understand that the Hebrew God, Yahweh, is the only true God and Creator of everything. Let Your will be done concerning this world and let your kingdom come soon, with Your kingdom comes world peace and true security. Thank You Lord for hearing this prayer, in the name of Jesus, Yeshua, the Messiah, Amen.

Posted by lance at 4:49 AM

Wednesday, March 30, 2011

SCRIPTURE FOR TODAY PROVERBS 11:8-9

"The righteous man is rescued from trouble, and it comes on the wicked instead. With his mouth the Godless destroys his neighbor, but through knowledge the righteous escape."

Posted by lance at 4:52 AM

PRAYER FOR FAMILY

Lord God, Yahweh, in Jesus' name I thank You for such a wonderful family, my children and grand children are my greatest joy and blessing. Help me Lord to help them understand how important it is to serve You and how simple it is to just "believe". Help me to be a good example to follow and let them know and have faith in You. Let them know the truth so that they can be set free from guilt and condemnation knowing that You sent Your one and only son as a sacrifice for us that we might be saved and have a place in Your kingdom forever. Help me to be a good teacher and share the knowledge and wisdom You have given me with them in a way they can understand. Thank You Lord, in the name of Jesus, Yeshua, the Messiah, Amen

Posted by lance at 4:48 AM

Thursday, March 31, 2011

SCRIPTURE FOR TODAY PROVERBS 3:13-18

"Blessed is the man who finds wisdom, the man who gains understanding, for she is more profitable than silver and yields better returns than gold. She is more precious than rubies; nothing you desire can compare with her. Long life is in her right hand; in her left hand are riches and honor. Her ways are pleasant ways and her paths are peace. She is a tree of life to those who embrace her; those that lay hold of her will be blessed."

Posted by lance at 5:01 AM

PRAYER FOR WISDOM

Lord God, Yahweh, Thank You for Your Word and for all the wisdom in it. Help me to build my life around it and share it with others, especially my family and friends. Lead me on a path to Your kingdom and help me to understand spiritual things so I can teach others what You have given us. Thank You for the Holy Spirit who is our guide and comforter in these last days. Help me to hear the voice of the Holy Spirit and let Him lead me in the way I should go according to Your Word, by the power of the Holy Spirit, in Jesus, Yeshua the Messiah's name, Amen.

Posted by lance at 4:50 AM

APRIL 2011

Friday, April 1, 2011

SCRIPTURE FOR TODAY PROVERBS 4:20-25

"My son, pay attention to what I say; listen closely to my words. Do not let them out of your sight, keep them within your heart; for they are life to those who find them and health to a man's whole body. Above all else guard your heart, for it is the well spring of life. put away perversity from your mouth; keep corrupt talk far from your lips. Let your eyes look straight ahead, fix your gaze directly before you."

Posted by lance at 4:53 AM

PRAYER FOR HEALING

Lord God, Yahweh, Thank You for sending Your son to save us from ourselves and to give us a way to get close to You, our source of everything. Help us to take Your word to heart and be a doer and believer of what You tell us. All things are possible with You if we only believe. You will help us if we put our faith in You. You will heal us, mind and body, if we let You. Thank You Lord, in Jesus name, Yeshua, the Messiah, Amen

Posted by lance at 4:45 AM

Saturday, April 2, 2011

SCRIPTURE FOR TODAY PROVERBS 2:6-11

"For the LORD gives wisdom, and from his mouth come knowledge and understanding. He holds victory in store for the upright, he is a shield to those whose walk is blameless, for he guards the course of the just and protects the way of his faithful ones."

"Then you will understand what is right and fair---every good path. For wisdom will enter your heart, and knowledge will be pleasant to your soul. Discretion will protect you and understanding will guard you."

Posted by lance at 8:14 PM

PRAYER FOR WISDOM

Lord God, Yahweh, Thank you for Your word and for teaching us the things we need to know to make our lives better and more joyful. Your wisdom is there for us to study and then to put into practice for our protection and benefit. Help me to show those around me the power and awesome truth of Your words and to be a positive influence to my family and friends and bring glory and honor to Your name by living by Your word. I need Your help every day to give me strength to do what I know is right and best even when my own thoughts are not what I want to think. Help me by the power of the Holy Spirit, in the name of Jesus, Yeshua, the Messiah. Amen

Posted by lance at 8:04 PM

Monday, April 4, 2011

SPECIAL PRAYER FOR "HEAVENBOUNDCAROL"

Father God, Yahweh, There is a family in danger of losing their home and living in their car, we ask that You move to bless them Lord, in their time of need and supply them with whatever resources they need to stay in their home. Bless them and comfort them by the power of the Holy Spirit in the name of Yeshua, Jesus, the Messiah. Amen

Posted by lance at 4:43 AM

SCRIPTURE FOR TODAY PROVERBS 1:7

"The fear of the LORD is the beginning of knowledge, but fools despise wisdom and discipline."

Posted by lance at 4:30 AM

PRAYER FOR RESISTING TEMPTATIONS

Father God, Yahweh, In Jesus, Yeshua's name I ask for strength in resisting certain temptations. Things I used to do and things I still would like to do that I know are displeasing to You. You know my weaknesses and habits, I need You to help me fight these things so I can be in Your favor and receive all the blessings You have for me. I'm sorry for the wrong things I do, please forgive me and help me to be the person You would like me to be, for my own good. And to bring glory and honor to Your name. Thank You for Your mercy and grace, according to Your word, in the name of Yeshua, Jesus, our Messiah. Make it so, Amen

Posted by lance at 4:26 AM

Tuesday, April 5, 2011

SCRIPTURE FOR TODAY PSALM 100:1-5

"Shout for joy to the LORD, all the earth. Worship the lord with gladness; come before him with joyful songs. Know that the LORD is God. It is he who made us and we are his; we are his people, the sheep of his pasture".

"Enter his gates with thanksgiving and his courts with praise; give thanks to him and praise his name. For the LORD is good and his love endures forever; his faithfulness continues through all generations".

Posted by lance at 4:15 AM

PRAYER FOR FRIENDS AND WORK MATES

Father God, Yahweh, Help me to share Your Word with my friends and the people I work with. Help me to conduct myself in a more proper way so people will know I follow You. I have certain things in my life I would like to change, bad language, stupid jokes, wrong thoughts. I am at Your mercy, Lord. I am a sinner and I need Your mercy and grace for my salvation. I am a believer and I love Your word, I just have a hard time trying to be without sin. I know that the blood of Jesus, Yeshua, washed away my sin. Thank You Lord, some people get the wrong idea about a person like me who believes. Some say I am hypocritical. I say I am only a man, a sinner who has faith in the saving power of the blood of our Messiah. I struggle with wrong thoughts and I need Your Holy Spirit to help me replace wrong thoughts with Your thoughts, Your Word. Thank You Lord, by the power of the Holy Spirit, according to Your Word, In the name of Jesus, make it so, Amen.

Posted by lance at 4:04 AM

Wednesday, April 6, 2011

SCRIPTURE FOR TODAY PSALMS 1:1-3

"Blessed is the man who does not walk in the counsel of the wicked or stand in the way of sinners or sit in the seat of mockers. But his delight is in the law of the LORD, and on His law he meditates day and night. He is like a tree planted by streams of water, which yields its fruit in season and whose leaf does not whither. Whatever he does prospers".

Posted by lance at 4:56 AM

PRAYER FOR SAFETY

Father God, Yahweh, Please watch over my family and keep us safe in these last days. Help us to understand what's happening to the world we live in and why. I know You are not happy with man in general and You are going to change things soon. I pray that You will protect us from all forms of sickness and accidents and attacks by the enemy. Lead us on a path to Your kingdom and let us know we are saved by our faith in Yeshua, Jesus, our Messiah. Help us to prepare for the hard times to come and bless us with provisions and resources to live in this world until You come back. According to your word, by the power of the Holy Spirit, in the name of Yeshua, Jesus , Amen.

Posted by lance at 4:50 AM

Thursday, April 7, 2011

SCRIPTURE FOR TODAY PSALMS 2:7-9

"I will proclaim the decree of the LORD:

"He said to me, "You are my son; today I have become your father. Ask of me, and I will make the nations your inheritance, the ends of the earth your possession. You will rule them with an iron scepter; you will dash them to pieces like pottery".

Posted by lance at 4:55 AM

PRAYER FOR TODAY

Father God, Yahweh, Thank You for being my God and creator, Thank You for Your mercy and grace and love. Forgive me for my selfish ways and help me to be more giving and compassionate. Bless me with wisdom and understanding that I might share with others and bring glory and honor to Your name. Help me to provide for my family in these last days and keep them safe and unharmed until we get to Your kingdom. You are an awesome Father, thank you for being close to me even when I do not deserve Your kindness. Help me to resist temptation and be a faithful servant for You. In Jesus name, Yeshua, our Messiah, Amen

Posted by lance at 4:49 AM

Friday, April 8, 2011

SCRIPTURE FOR TODAY JAMES 4:7-9

"Be patient, then, brothers, until the Lords coming. See how the farmer waits for the land to yield its valuable crop and how patient he is for the autumn and spring rains. You too, be patient and stand firm, because the Lords coming is near. Don't grumble against each other, brothers, or you will be judged. The judge is standing at the door"!

Posted by lance at 4:57 AM

PRAYER TO GIVE THANKS FOR ANSWERED PRAYERS

Father God, Yahweh, Thank You for answering so many of my prayers. It's awesome to have a God like You who loves me and is not partial but treats us all the same who loves You and your Word. Thank You for being my "Abba" Father and help me to draw more people to You in these last days according to Your Word. Thank You for the fruits of the Holy Spirit which are, love, joy, and peace, kindness mildness faithfulness, patience, self control and goodness. Thank You for helping me grow in these things. In the name of Jesus, Yeshua, our savior, Amen

Posted by lance at 4:48 AM

Sunday, April 10, 2011

SCRIPTURE FOR TODAY JAMES 5:13-16

"Is anyone of you in trouble? He should pray. Is anyone happy? Let him sing songs of praise. Is anyone of you sick? He should call the elders of the church to pray over him and anoint him with oil in the name of the Lord. And the prayer offered in faith will make the sick person well; the Lord will raise him up. If he has sinned he will be forgiven. Therefore confess your sins to each other and pray for each other so that you may be healed. The prayer of a righteous man is powerful and effective".

Posted by lance at 3:25 PM

PRAYER FOR SOMEONE IN TROUBLE

Father God, Yahweh, I need You to help me with a situation I find myself in. Lord, I know I made a mistake and used bad judgment and now I'm in some trouble. I need You to help me through this and strengthen me to get over it. I know I was wrong, I just pray my punishment will be lenient and over as soon as possible. I do repent and ask for forgiveness from all concerned. If there is any way to avoid this help me find it and have justice or compromise. I am not perfect and tend to make mistakes and bad judgment calls. That does not hold me back from believing in You and trusting in You. Thank You for being my God and Savior. In the name of Yeshua, Jesus, Our Messiah, according to Your Word, make it so, Amen.

Posted by lance at 3:16 PM

Monday, April 11, 2011

SCRIPTURE FOR TODAY COLOSSIANS 1:9-10

"For this reason, since the day we heard about you, we have not stopped praying for you and asking God to fill you with the knowledge of his will through all spiritual wisdom and understanding. And we pray this that you may live a life worthy of the Lord and may please him in every way: bearing fruit in every good work, growing in the knowledge of God,"

Posted by lance at 4:38 AM

PRAYER FOR TODAY

Father God, Yahweh, Thank You for this day Lord and all the blessings in my life. Help me to be a better person day by day and please forgive my sins and wrong thoughts. Help me to be more obedient and behave as a follower of our Lord, Yeshuah, Jesus, our savior. Lord, I know I am a sinful man and I need Your mercy and grace for my salvation. I want to serve You Lord, help me to be a faithful follower and do Your Word not just hear it. Thank You Lord, for answering so many of my prayers. Please help me to resist the temptations that come on me. Thank You. In the name of Jesus, Yeshua, the Messiah, by the power of the Holy Spirit, Amen.

Posted by lance at 4:30 AM

Tuesday, April 12, 2011

ANOTHER THOUGHT TO SHARE

I've come to the conclusion that most of the noted T.V. evangelists are really sincere in what they do. Some preach prosperity gospels, others fire and brimstone, still others share wisdom from the scriptures and then there is the salvation by grace and so on. Not all of them are "out for the money" most use the money they receive for doing God's work which does cost money. Preaching to the world about the good news is expensive and a lot of work. God blesses people who do his will. His will is to preach The Good News, which is the Gospel. So, if they are prosperous it's because they are blessed for doing what God wants them to do. Joyce Meyer, John Hagee, The 700 Club with Pat Robertson and some others are successful for a reason. If they were frauds they would have been exposed by now and brought to ruin. But they are thriving. Why? They are doing God's work by the power of the Holy Spirit.

They all have a certain message to share and focus on to teach us, put them all together and you have the "truth" that we all need to hear, the "Good News" is, we are all saved by the grace of God if we believe and if we are willing to receive the free gift of God, which is the good and acceptable will of our heavenly Father God, salvation and forgiveness by our Lord Jesus the Christ! It's all about Jesus!!! Lance

Posted by lance at 9:47 PM

A THOUGHT TO SHARE

I have been a believer for a long time but never really knew the power that is available to us through our prayers. I used to think that because I was a "sinner" God would not listen to me. I smoked and drank and did things that most "sinners" do not realizing that I was just the one God was looking for. He was willing to take me in just the way I was and make me His son and give me His love despite my sinful nature.

Having Jesus in my life has made a huge difference in my way of thinking, even though I am still a work in progress I have full faith that someday I will become the man I've always wanted to be. My main goal in this life is to follow Christ and be a blessing to my family and friends despite my imperfections and sinful nature. As I grow in Gods wisdom and truth my life is changing for the best before my eyes, although I have moments of weakness and bad judgment calls I still hold firm to the truth that's sets us free. That truth is the good news, The Gospel message found in God's Word. John 3:16 The free gift of eternal life by Gods grace alone, not by things we do or don't do but by Gods undeserved kindness. We need only to accept Jesus as our savior, admit to our sinful nature, and receive the forgiveness and love he has for us. Lance

Posted by lance at 6:54 PM

SCRIPTURE FOR TODAY PROVERBS 17:28

"Even a fool is thought wise if he keeps silent, and discerning if he holds his tongue."

Posted by lance at 4:55 AM

PRAYER FOR TODAY

Father God, Yahweh, Thank You for wisdom in handling certain problems that come up in life. I know I need Your word to guide me through these tough times. Help me to be a blessing to my family and friends and share Your wisdom with them every chance I get. Forgive me for my sins and help me to resist temptation and be a better man. Thank You Lord, In the name of Yeshua, Jesus, our Savior, Amen.

Posted by lance at 4:52 AM

Wednesday, April 13, 2011

SCRIPTURE FOR TODAY PHILIPPIANS 3:12-15

"Not that I have already obtained all this, or have already been made perfect, but I press on to take hold of that for which Christ Jesus took hold of me. Brothers, I do not consider myself yet to take hold of it. But one thing I do: Forgetting what is behind and straining toward what is ahead, I press on toward the goal to win the prize for which God Has called me heavenward in Christ Jesus."

"All of us who are mature should take such a view of things. And if on some point you think differently, that too God will make clear to you."

Posted by lance at 6:58 AM

PRAYER FOR TODAY

Lord God, Yahweh, I thank You Lord for Your mercy and grace. For forgiveness of my sins and for being my God and heavenly Father. For forgetting what is behind me and helping me to find peace and joy now by the power of the Holy Spirit. Even though I will stumble and fall many times I have faith that You are there to catch me and comfort me with Your Word. You will wipe the tears from my eyes and lead me on a path to Your kingdom. Help me to share Your Word and wisdom with others and lead them on a path to You. Thank You Lord, In the name of Yeshua, Jesus, the Messiah, Amen, by the power of the Holy Spirit.

Posted by lance at 6:48 AM

Thursday, April 14, 2011

SCRIPTURE FOR TODAY JOHN 20:30-31

"Jesus did many other miraculous signs in the presence of his disciples, which are not recorded in this book. But these are written that you may believe that Jesus is the Christ, the Son of God, and that by believing you may have life in his name."

Posted by lance at 4:56 AM

PRAYER FOR TODAY

Father God, Yahweh, Thank You , Thank You, Thank You, Thank You, a million thanks to You Lord for watching over me and answering my prayers. Despite my sinful nature You are still guiding me and protecting me against the enemy. Despite my stubbornness You are still with me. You work in marvelous ways. Help me to bring glory and honor to Your name. I pray that You watch over my children and grand children also in these last days and keep them all safe and happy by the power of the Holy Spirit, according to your word, in the name of Yeshua, Jesus, our Savior and Lord, Amen

Posted by lance at 4:45 AM

Friday, April 15, 2011

SCRIPTURE FOR TODAY JOHN 21:25

"Jesus did many other things as well. If every one of them were written down, I suppose that even the whole world would not have room for the books that would be written."

Posted by lance at 4:32 AM

PRAYER FOR TODAY

Father God, Yahweh, Help me Father to get through these hard times and help me to avoid trouble. I only want peace and joy in my life and I know that this kind peace and joy can only come with your blessings. Bless me Lord so that I can be a blessing and inspire others to want to know and serve you the only true God, there is none other. I love You Lord and I love Your Word, thank You for forgiving me each day for the things I do wrong and for the wrong thoughts I think. Help me to control myself in all things and bring glory and honor to your name. Be with me Lord and protect me from my enemies and the enemy of us all. In the name of Yeshua, Jesus, our Savior, Amen

Posted by lance at 4:26 AM

Saturday, April 16, 2011

SPECIAL SCRIPTURE FOR ISRAEL PSALM 114

"When Israel came out of Egypt, the house of Jacob from a people with a foreign tongue, Judah became God's sanctuary, Israel his dominion. The sea looked and fled, the Jordan turned back; the mountains skipped like rams, the hill like lambs. Tremble, O earth, at the presence of the LORD, at the presence of the God of Jacob, who turned the rock into a pool, the hard rock into springs of water".

Posted by lance at 9:59 AM

SPECIAL PRAYER FOR ISRAEL

Lord God, Yahweh, God of Abraham, Isaac, and Jacob, Strengthen your people Father God against the enemies that seek to destroy Your people and their land that You have given them. Be with them and guide the leaders of Your nation Israel. Let them know that You will protect them with Your mighty hand and crush the enemies that come against them according to Your Word and Your promises. Bless Israel Father God and let them shine as a people surrounded by their enemies as You make known to the world that no weapon formed against them will work and that You personally are their protector according to Your Word, in the name of Yeshua, Jesus, our Messiah and Savior, Amen.

Posted by lance at 9:50 AM

SCRIPTURE FOR TODAY GALATIANS 5: 22-26

"But the fruit of the Spirit is love , joy, peace, patience, kindness, goodness, faithfulness, gentleness and self control. Against such things there is no law. Those who belong to Christ Jesus have crucified the sinful nature with its passions and desires. Since we live by the Spirit, let us keep in step with the Spirit. Let us not become conceited, provoking and envying each other".

Posted by lance at 8:33 AM

PRAYER FOR TODAY

Father God, Yahweh, Thank You Lord for the Holy Spirit that comforts us and guides us through this life. Help me to know when He is talking to me and lead me to do what I'm told for my own good so I can show myself a believer and follower of our Lord Jesus. Bless me Lord, with all the fruits of the Spirit, love, joy, peace, kindness, gentleness, faithfulness, patience, self control, and goodness. Bless me also with wisdom so that I will make better decisions and judgment calls. I ask only for a happy and secure, prosperous life here and now and a place in Your kingdom when I leave this world. Help me to be a better man and a blessing to my children and grandchildren, friends and family and people I don't even know. In the name of Yeshua, Jesus, our Lord and Savior, Amen.

Posted by lance at 8:24 AM

Sunday, April 17, 2011

SCRIPTURE FOR TODAY PSALM 115:1-3

"Not to us, O LORD, not to us but to Your name be the glory, because of your love and faithfulness.

Why do the nations say, "Where is their God?" Our God is in heaven; he does whatever pleases him."

Posted by lance at 8:39 AM

PRAYER FOR TODAY

Father God, Yahweh, Thank You Lord for your mercy and grace and loving kindness towards Your people. I know you created us with a plan and purpose and that you only want the best for all of us. Help me to be a person after Your own heart and bless me with love , joy , peace and prosperity that I might bring glory and honor to Your name in these last days until You set up Your kingdom on earth and bring true and lasting peace for all of us who believe. Your Word tells us all we need to know and I will keep trying to understand everything You have told us. The main thing I have learned is that You don't want us to be afraid of what's happening now and that we should all keep praying for the peace of Jerusalem. And that we should love our neighbors as ourselves according to Your word in Jesus, Yeshua's name, Amen

Posted by lance at 8:34 AM

Monday, April 18, 2011

SCRIPTURE FOR TODAY PSALM 112:1-5

"Praise the LORD". "Blessed is the man who fears the LORD, who finds great delight in his commands.

His children will be mighty in the land; the generation of the upright will be blessed. Wealth and riches are in his house, and his righteousness endures forever. Even in the darkness light dawns for the upright, for the gracious and compassionate and righteous man. Good will come to him who is generous and lends freely, who conducts his affairs with justice".

Posted by lance at 4:53 AM

PRAYER FOR TODAY

Father God, Yahweh, I pray that You will watch over my children and grandchildren in these last days and protect them from all forms of sickness and disease and accidents. Keep them safe and lead them on a path to your kingdom. Help me to share your word with them and be a better influence on them. In the past I have not been as good a person as I could have been, help me to be better and be a great blessing to them. Help me every day to do your will in this life because I believe what you say in your word. I thank You for your mercy and grace without it I would not make it to your kingdom. I pray for the peace of Jerusalem and protection for your people around the world. In the name of Yeshua, Jesus , our Messiah, by the power of the Holy Spirit, and according to your Word, Amen

Posted by lance at 4:44 AM

Tuesday, April 19, 2011

MATTHEW 7:7-8

"Ask and it will be given to you; seek and you will find; knock and the door will be open to you. For everyone who asks receives; he who seeks finds; and to him who knocks the door will be opened."

Posted by lance at 4:57 AM

PRAYER FOR TODAY

Father God, Yahweh, Thank You Lord for divine creativity and ideas that will bring prosperity and security to my family and break the curse of lack and poverty. Thank You Lord that we have more than just enough so that we can give and share with others and bring glory and honor to your name and experience the joy of giving. Protect us in these last days as we prepare for your coming and help us to have a better understanding of your word, in the name of Yeshua, Jesus, our Savior, according to your word. Amen

Posted by lance at 4:51 AM

Wednesday, April 20, 2011

SCRIPTURE FOR TODAY ROMANS 4:7-8

"Blessed are they whose transgressions are forgiven, whose sins are covered. Blessed is the man whose sin the Lord will never count against him".

Posted by lance at 4:49 AM

PRAYER FOR TODAY

Father God, Yahweh, Thank You for your Word that comforts us and gives us hope in these last days that we who believe will be saved and made new by the power of the Holy Spirit. That we will have everlasting life in your kingdom and a better life here and now. You are our Mighty God, Prince of Peace, and Wonderful Councilor. Thank you for your undeserved kindness and unconditional love as a parent loves his children so the same way you love us. Help me to do things to make you proud of me and not disappointed. Forgive me for my sins and help me to do good not bad. Thank You Lord for always hearing my prayers. By the power of the Holy Spirit, according to your Word, in the name of Yeshua, Jesus, our Savior, Amen.

Posted by lance at 4:44 AM

Thursday, April 21, 2011

SPECIAL PRAYER FOR RANDY H.

Lord God, Yahweh, in the name Jesus I pray for a fellow worker who was just diagnosed with stage 4 cancer throughout his body. Father, I ask that You comfort him if this is your will and if You are calling him home to you. Lord God help him to know that he is forgiven and his name is written in the Lambs "Book of Life" I also pray that all of his family members, that You are comforting them as we pray. Make Randy's last days in this life as joyful and as painless as possible. In the name of Jesus, Yeshua, our Lord and Savior. Amen.

Posted by lance at 7:57 PM

SCRIPTURE FOR TODAY ROMANS 5:1-4

"Therefore, since we have been justified through faith, we have peace with God through our Lord Jesus Christ, through whom we have gained access by faith into this grace in which we now stand. And we rejoice in the hope of the glory of God. Not only so, but we also rejoice in our sufferings, because we know that our suffering produces perseverance; character; and character, Hope."

Posted by lance at 4:32 AM

PRAYER FOR TODAY

Father God, Yahweh, Help me to find favor with You today concerning problems that have come up. I know that all things are possible with you and that You can make all things turn out for good. You know the problems I face and I know You will help if I ask, thank You Lord for helping me. I thank You for being there for me when I need You. Help me to do your will and protect me from all enemies and help me to be a better influence on the people I love. Forgive me for all of my sins. I pray for the peace of Jerusalem and protection for your people around the world. According to your Word, by the power of the Holy Ghost, in the name of Yeshua, Jesus, our savior, Amen.

Posted by lance at 4:22 AM

Friday, April 22, 2011

GOOD FRIDAY PRAYER

Lord God, Yahweh, Thank You for the great sacrifice that You gave so that our sins would be forgiven and that we can stand before You blameless though our sins be as scarlet we are made white as snow by the power of the blood of Your Son, Yeshuah, Jesus, our Lord and Savior. The Lamb of God that takes away the sins of the world! Thank You Lord Jesus, Yeshua, For dying for me, for suffering the way You did for me, for the beating and the humiliation that should have been meant for me, I thank You Lord! You are awesome Lord! Please forgive me for my weakness and help me be strong. I love You Jesus and I love Your word. Thank You, Thank You, 1000 times. I need You Lord Jesus. Come into my life and stay with me. By the power of the Holy Spirit, According to Your word, In the name of Yeshua, Jesus, my Savior and God, Amen.

Posted by lance at 6:35 PM

SCRIPTURE FOR TODAY 1JOHN5:13-15

"I write these things to you who believe in the name of the son of God so that you may know that you have eternal life. This is the confidence we have in approaching God: that if we ask anything according to his will, he hears us. And if we know that he hears us--whatever we ask--we know that we will have what we ask of him."

Posted by lance at 4:49 AM

PRAYER FOR TODAY

Lord God ,Yahweh, Help me Lord not to fear the trouble that is upon me. My trouble is like nothing compared to some other people I know. Your Word says, "Fear not", Father God, help me to get through this and be stronger because of it. You are my shield and my refuge, what can man do to me? This will pass and I will be better for it. I pray for strength and faith that I will overcome the fear that is in me.

Lord I pray for the peace of Jerusalem and protection for Your people around the world. By the power of the Holy Spirit, according to Your word, in the name of Jesus, Yeshua, our Lord and Savior, Amen.

Posted by lance at 4:42 AM

Saturday, April 23, 2011

WHAT IS THE "GOSPEL?"

The meaning of the word "Gospel" is simply "Good News". What is the good news that the Word of God is talking about? Well, what is the "best" news a mortal person could ever hear? Come on, think about it. What is the best news a human being could ever hear? It is this; "to live forever" in peace and harmony with God, forgiven of all your sins, help for the asking, for prosperity and abundance in this life, comfort, wisdom, joy, and peace. The "Good News" is that Jesus, Yeshua, in his language, was Gods son, and still is. Imagine, if you will, what it would be like to watch your child die. Our God did. So that we would be forgiven of the sin that prevents us from fellowship with him. Jesus, Yeshua, was the sacrificial lamb of Yahweh, the Creator of heaven and earth, His own Son!! Think about it!!

How much do you love God? Would you do what He did for, anything?

God must be love. I choose love and life, God is good all the time, Thank You God for being who You are!

Posted by lance at 8:48 PM

SCRIPTURE FOR TODAY JOHN 14:15-18

"If you love me, you will obey what I command. And I will ask the Father and He will give you another Counselor to be with you forever---the Spirit of Truth. The world cannot accept him, because it neither sees him nor knows him. But you know him, for he lives with you and will be in you. I will not leave you as orphans; I will come to you."

Posted by lance at 6:41 AM

PRAYER FOR TODAY

Father God, Yahweh, Thank You for this day that You have made. Thank You for all my blessings. For my health, my children and grand children who bring me great joy, for my job that buys us food and pays the bills, for my friends who are there for me when I need help and that I can help them when they are in need. Thank You that I have more than enough so that I can give to those in lack. Thank You for your Word that guides me and the Holy Spirit that comforts me. Help me to count all my blessings and be grateful to You Lord God and obey what You want me to do so that I can experience all the good things You have in store for me. Help me to get closer to You and grow spiritually and share the knowledge and wisdom with all who want to hear and even some who may not want to hear it. Thank You, in the name of Jesus, Yeshua, our Lord and Savior, Amen.

Posted by lance at 6:21 AM

Sunday, April 24, 2011

SCRIPTURE FOR TODAY MARK 16:6-7

"Don't be alarmed", he said. "You are looking for Jesus the Nazarene, who was crucified. He has risen! He is not here. See the place where they laid him. But go, tell his disciples and Peter, He is going ahead of you into Galilee. There you will see him, just as he told you".

Posted by lance at 10:03 AM

PRAYER FOR TODAY

Father God, Yahweh, Thank You for another day of life and all the blessings that go with it. Thank You for watching over me and my family in these last days. I pray for wisdom and guidance by the power of the Holy Ghost to get through the hard times to come. Help me to do Your will Lord because I know that it is right and beneficial for my life. I only want peace, love, joy, and prosperity for myself and family and a place in Your Kingdom when this system of things is brought to an end. I thank You for being my God and saving me from eternal destruction. Thank You Father, for raising Yeshua, Jesus, from the dead and giving us the hope and promise of everlasting life with You in peace and joy and perfect love. Thank You. In the name of Jesus, Yeshua, our Lord and Savior, Amen.

Posted by lance at 9:54 AM

Monday, April 25, 2011

SCRIPTURE FOR TODAY MARK 13:5-8

"Jesus said to them": "Watch out that no one deceives you. Many will come in my name claiming, "I am he", and will deceive many. When you hear of wars and rumors of wars, do not be alarmed. Such things must happen, but the end is still to come. Nation will rise against nation, and kingdom against kingdom. There will be earthquakes in various places, and famines. These are the beginning of birth pains".

Posted by lance at 5:05 AM

PRAYER FOR TODAY

Father God, Yahweh, Please help me to better provide for my family. Lord, I want to help my kids more with all their needs. I want to be in a position to help them with whatever they want and need. I want to help make their lives as comfortable and secure as possible. I also want to teach them to come to you in prayer for the things they want and need. I confess and regret I didn't really know You when they were growing up and so they were not taught spiritual things the way they should have been, by my example. Help me to make up for that now. Times are hard and getting worse Lord, as You predicted. Watch over us in these last days and keep us safe and unharmed until You come back in all Your glory. In the name of Yeshua, Jesus, our Messiah and Savior, and according to Your Word. Amen.

Posted by lance at 4:51 AM

Tuesday, April 26, 2011

PRAYER FOR TODAY

Lord God, Yahweh, In Jesus name, Forgive me for my sins and help me through this day. By the power of the Holy Spirit, according to Your word, Amen.

Posted by lance at 4:59 AM

SCRIPTURE FOR TODAY JAMES 5-13-16

"Is any one of you in trouble? He should pray. Is anyone happy? Let him sing songs of praise. Is any one of you sick? He should call the elders of the church to pray over him and anoint him with oil in the name of the Lord. And the prayer offered in faith will make the sick person well; the Lord will raise him up. If he has sinned, he will be forgiven. Therefore confess your sins to each other so that you may be healed. The prayer of a righteous man is powerful and effective".

Posted by lance at 4:53 AM

Wednesday, April 27, 2011

SCRIPTURE FOR TODAY COLOSSIANS 3:1-3

"Since, then, you have been raised with Christ, set your hearts on things above, where Christ is seated at the right hand of God. Set your minds on things above, not on earthly things. For you died and your life is now hidden with Christ in God".

Posted by lance at 4:54 AM

PRAYER FOR TODAY

Father God, Yahweh, Why do I have to be who I am and do the things I do knowing that I do wrong? Even though I really don't want to do the things I do that I know are not right. I seem to have no control over what I do even after I ask You for self control. All I can do is to ask You to forgive me and have mercy on me and have faith that You will forgive my sins. Help me to be a better person and a light to those around me. Help me to do your will and have a place in Your kingdom. Help me to be a better example to my children and grandchildren. I pray for the peace of Jerusalem, In the name of Jesus, according to Your word, by the power of the Holy Spirit, Amen.

Posted by lance at 4:46 AM

Thursday, April 28, 2011

SCRIPTURE FOR TODAY COLOSSIANS 2:1-3

"I urge, then, first of all, that requests, prayers, intersession and thanksgiving be made for everyone---for kings and all those in authority, that we may live peaceful and quiet lives in all godliness and holiness. This is good and pleases God our Savior,"

Posted by lance at 4:48 AM

PRAYER FOR TODAY

Father God, Yahweh, Help me today to get by this worry I'm dealing with. Help me to overcome the fear that I feel. Your Word Says, "Fear not". Help me to be at ease and get over all this trouble. Help me to get some good news today so I can rest and get back to normal. Thank You Lord for all my blessings and especially for being my God and Savior. In the name Jesus, Yeshua, by the power of the Holy Ghost, Amen.

Posted by lance at 4:42 AM

Friday, April 29, 2011

SCRIPTURE FOR TODAY 1 TIMOTHY 4:1-5

"The Spirit clearly says that in the latter times some will abandon the faith and follow deceiving spirits and things taught by demons. Such teachings come through hypocritical liars, whose consciences have been seared as with a hot iron. They forbid people to marry and order them to abstain from certain foods, which God created to be received with thanksgiving by those who believe and know the truth, for everything God created is good, and nothing is to be rejected if it is received with thanksgiving, because it is consecrated by the word of God and prayer."

Posted by lance at 4:57 AM

PRAYER FOR TODAY

Father God, Yahweh, Thank You for another day of life and a another chance to do good and to bring glory and honor to your name. I'm sorry for my sins and help me to be a better person. Help me to be a good role model for my grand children and a better friend to my friends. Bless me with resources that I can share with others when the times get really bad. Lord God I thank You for your word that gives us knowledge and wisdom and for the Holy Spirit that comforts us in our trials and hardships. Please give me courage and strength in these last days to make it till the end. Thank You Lord God, in the name of Jesus, Yeshua, our Savior, Amen.

Posted by lance at 4:47 AM

Saturday, April 30, 2011

SCRIPTURE FOR TODAY 1 THESSALONIANS 4:13-18

"Brothers we do not want you to be ignorant about those who fall asleep or to grieve like the rest of men, who have no hope. We believe that Jesus died and rose again and so we believe that God will bring with Jesus those who have fallen asleep in Him. According to the Lord's own word, we tell you that we who are still alive, who are left till the coming of the Lord, will certainly not precede those who have fallen asleep. For the Lord himself will come down from heaven, with a loud command, with the voice of the archangel and with the trumpet call of God, and the dead in Christ will rise first. After that, we who are still alive and left will be caught up together with them in the clouds to meet the Lord in the air. And so we will be with the Lord forever. Therefore, encourage each other with these words."

Posted by lance at 8:21 AM

PRAYER FOR TODAY

Lord God, Yahweh, Thank You for all my blessings Lord. Help me to be a better person, Strengthen my faith in Your word every day with answers to my prayers. Help me to be a better provider for my family and a better friend to my friends. Help me to be a better more generous giver to those in need and to ministries who help those in need. Lord, I'm sorry for my sins and I ask for forgiveness for all that I do wrong. Help me to use better judgment in all things that I do and give me wisdom to make important decisions. Bless me with all the fruits of the Holy Spirit and health and prosperity. I pray for the peace of Jerusalem, according to Your Word, in the name of Yeshua, Jesus, our Lord and Savior, Amen.

Posted by lance at 8:03 AM

MAY 2011

Sunday, May 1, 2011

PRAYER FOR DIVINE CREATIVITY

Father God, Yahweh, I ask in prayer for divine creativity. An idea that I can make work with your help to achieve financial prosperity and freedom from lack and poverty, not just for me but for all those I love and care about and even for some that don't know me. I just feel like I'm not doing enough and really don't know what to do. That's why I'm asking for your help with a way to bless others as you bless me. I don't know how you will do it, I just know that you will because your word says that you will give us the desires of our hearts if we only believe and have faith that you will. I will be patiently waiting for the gift of divine creativity, for the Idea I can use to change my life and the lives of my loved ones for the better and to bring glory and honor to your name, in the name of Yeshua, Jesus, our Lord and Savior, according to your Word, Amen

Posted by lance at 7:25 PM

SCRIPTURE FOR TODAY COLOSSIANS 1:15-17

"He is the image of the invisible God, the firstborn over all creation. For by Him all things were created: things in heaven and on earth, visible and invisible, whether thrones or powers or authorities; all things were created by him and for him. He is before all things, and in him all things hold together."

Posted by lance at 11:41 AM

PRAYER FOR TODAY

Father God, Yahweh, Today I praise your name for being a God of Love and for making a way for us where there seems to be no way. Thank You for sacrificing Your one and only son so that we might live forever in paradise with You in your glory. You are the only true God, there is no other. There is no other way to life everlasting, It's all about life and love and peace and Joy unspeakable. Fill me with your Word and make me a new creature. Thank You, Lord God, for wisdom and truth and the hope of everlasting life according to your Word, in the name of Jesus, Yeshua, our Lord and Savior. Amen

Posted by lance at 11:32 AM

Monday, May 2, 2011

SCRIPTURE FOR TODAY PSALM 14:1-2

"The fool says in his heart, "There is no God". They are corrupt, their deeds are vile; there is no one who does good."

"The LORD looks down from heaven on the sons of men to see if there are any who understand, any who seek God."

Posted by lance at 4:57 AM

PRAYER FOR TODAY

Lord God, Yahweh, Thank You for another day of life a chance to make You proud. I know that you love me unconditionally and nothing I can do would hinder that love or make it any stronger but I just wish I could be a better man in your eyes, a creation to be proud of. As I am now I leave a lot to be desired but I can feel You working in me and that I am getting better in every way. Make me a better Christian, follower of Yeshua, Jesus. Help me to do His word and share with others without fear of what they might think. I know the truth about the good news, Gospel. Help me to share that with others. Please bless me with all the fruits of the Holy Spirit that I might shine in the darkness of this world, according to your word, by the power of the Holy Spirit, In the name of Yeshua, Jesus, Amen.

Posted by lance at 4:50 AM

Tuesday, May 3, 2011

SCRIPTURE FOR TODAY PSALM 18:-16

"He reached down from on high and took hold of me; he drew me out of deep waters. He rescued me from my powerful enemy, from my foes who were too strong for me. They confronted me in the day of my disaster, but the LORD was my support."

Posted by lance at 4:47 AM

PRAYER FOR TODAY

Father God, Yahweh, Help me Lord God to tell the difference between those who would hurt me and belittle me and those who would help me and encourage me. Help me to tell the difference between people who have good hearts and those who have not so good hearts, who want to know You and your word and those who do not want to know who You are. According to your word, I want to do what You say, talk about Jesus and spread the Gospel as best I can. I know I'm a sinner and need your mercy and grace, which is undeserved kindness and love. Help me to be a better believer and more obedient to Your word. Forgive me for my sin and help me to have self control, especially control over my mouth. Thank You Lord God, for hearing my prayers and for all my blessings. In the name of Jesus, Yeshua, my Lord and Savior, Amen

Posted by lance at 4:42 AM

Wednesday, May 4, 2011

SCRIPTURE FOR TODAY JOHN 15:18-19

"If the world hates you, keep in mind that it hated me first. If you belonged to the world it would love you as its own. As it is, you do not belong to the world, but I have chosen you out of the world. That is why the world hates you."

Posted by lance at 4:55 AM

PRAYER FOR TODAY

Father God, Yahweh, Thank You for being my God and Savior. Thank You for wisdom. I ask for all the fruits of the Holy Spirit to be evident in my life. I ask for protection for my family and myself in these last days as we see your prophesy's coming true before our eyes. Help me to spread your Gospel with courage and conviction so that people will know that your Word is true. So that many will come to you in these last days and be saved from the coming destruction. Bring us out of the trouble that is here now and getting worse. Thank You Lord for being the God that You are. You are the creator God, our Father and there is no other. According to your word, by the power of the Holy Spirit, in the name of Yeshua, Jesus, our Lord, Amen.

Posted by lance at 4:47 AM

Thursday, May 5, 2011

SCRIPTURE FOR TODAY LUKE 12:8-10

"I tell you, whoever acknowledges me before men, the Son of Man will acknowledge him before the angels of God. But he who disowns me before men will be disowned before the angels of God. And everyone who speaks a word against the Son of Man will be forgiven, but anyone who blasphemes against the Holy Spirit will not be forgiven."

Posted by lance at 4:54 AM

PRAYER FOR TODAY

Lord God, Yahweh, Father, today I come to you in prayer to ask for a better job. I know the job I'm on now is a blessing but its unhealthy, I've been breathing dirty air with lots of contaminates in it. Please help me to get on a cleaner job, outside in the fresh air like I'm used to. I know You hear my request and if it be Your will please make it so. Father , I also ask that You send angels to watch over my children and grandchildren in these last days and keep them safe and happy until Your kingdom comes and help me to be a blessing to all of them, now, and in the future. I pray for peace in Jerusalem and in Israel and Your wisdom for her leaders. Protect Your people around the world, In the name of Jesus, Yeshua, our Lord and Messiah, by the power of the Holy Spirit, Amen.

Posted by lance at 4:43 AM

Friday, May 6, 2011

SCRIPTURE FOR TODAY ISAIAH 46:8-10

"Remember this, fix it in your mind, take it to heart, you rebels. Remember the former things, those of long ago; I am God, and there is no other; I am God and there is none like me. I make known the end from the beginning, from ancient times, what is still to come. I say: "My purpose will stand, and I will do all that I please."

Posted by lance at 4:58 AM

PRAYER FOR TODAY

Father God, Yahweh, Thank You for wisdom and knowledge that I get from Your word. Thank You for being my God and my Father. Help me to be a son to be proud of. Bless me with love , joy, peace and all the fruits of the Holy Spirit. Help me to be bold when I share your Word with others and bring glory and honor to your name. I'm sorry for my sins and I ask forgiveness for them all and help me to turn away from temptation and be a better person in these last days. Help me to be a great blessing to my children and grandchildren and provide for them in these tough times. Thank You Lord for always hearing my prayers, in the name of Yeshua, Jesus, by the power of the Holy Spirit, according to your Word, Amen.

Posted by lance at 4:50 AM

Saturday, May 7, 2011

SCRIPTURE FOR TODAY ISAIAH 46:12-13

"Listen to me, you stubborn-hearted, you who are far from righteousness. I am bringing my righteousness near, it is not far away; and my salvation will not be delayed. I will grant salvation to Zion, my splendor to Israel."

Posted by lance at 7:58 AM

PRAYER FOR TODAY

Father God, Yahweh, Help me to have Joy and peace in my heart and mind, help me to be happy despite what's going on in the world and even around my own community. People are in fear more and more and because most don't know the reason for the fear because most don't know your Word and what it says about the last days. Thank You Lord for giving us believers a way out where there seems to be no way, Thank you for the hope we find in Your Word, the advanced warning we get when we study and pray and listen to your humble servants deliver to us the messages you want us to know. Father, help me to be a better witness to Your Word and do your will all I can. Forgive me for my sins and short comings let your mercy and grace be on me and bless me with all the fruits of the Holy Spirit. In the name of Yeshua, Jesus, by the power of the Holy Spirit, make it so, Amen

Posted by lance at 7:50 AM

Sunday, May 8, 2011

SPECIAL PRAYER FOR "MOTHERS"

Lord God Yahweh, Thank You Lord for all the Mothers of the world who give their love to their children and who sacrifice all for the well being of their sons and daughters. Bless them Father with all the joy and peace that their hearts can hold. Let the children honor them with praise and hugs and kisses today and every day. Let us not forget them in their old age and help them with whatever they need to the best of our ability, according to your word. Let us show our respect in every way and bless them with kind words and smiles. Thank You Father, for our Mothers, in the name of Jesus, Yeshua, Amen.

Posted by lance at 9:37 AM

SCRIPTURE FOR TODAY ISAIAH 49:8

"This is what the LORD says:" "In the time of my favor I will answer you, and in the day of salvation I will help you; I will keep you, and make you to be a covenant for the people, to restore the land and to reassign its desolate inheritances, to say to the captives, "Come out," and to those in darkness, "Be free!""

Posted by lance at 9:26 AM

PRAYER FOR TODAY

Lord God, Yahweh, Thank you Father for your prophets who let us know in advance what will happen on this earth according to your will and purpose. Help us to prepare and be ready for the trouble that will come upon this earth. I know that whatever happens is necessary and is in your good and perfect will. Thank you for warning us and helping us to get ready and bringing out of all the trouble. Bless me Lord with the ability to provide greatly for all those I love and even some I don't know. Help me to be a better giver and more tolerant of those who just don't understand or just don't want to hear the things we all need to know. Father forgive me for my sins and selfish nature and help me be a better man and follower of Jesus. Thank You for all my blessings in the name of Jesus, Yeshua, by the power of the Holy Spirit, according to your Word, Amen.

Posted by lance at 9:11 AM

Monday, May 9, 2011

SCRIPTURE FOR TODAY PSALM 37:7-9

"Be still before the LORD and wait patiently for him; do not fret when men succeed in their ways, when they carry out their wicked schemes. Refrain from anger and turn from wrath; do not fret---it leads only to evil. For evil men will be cut off, but those who hope in the LORD will inherit the land."

Posted by lance at 4:52 AM

PRAYER FOR TODAY

Father God Yahweh, Thank You Father for this day, let me rejoice and be glad in it, despite the trouble in the world and in my life. I know this trouble will pass soon and I will have peace and joy. Help me to get over this condition I have with my lungs, the cough and shortness of breath. Help me to find a new way to make a living, something I will enjoy and want to do. And make more money doing. I want to provide for my family in a big way, not just get by, but have more than enough so Ill have more to share and give to others. Bless my children and grandchildren with wisdom and good health and a place in your kingdom now and in the future. Forgive me for my sins and help me to be a better person and follower of Yeshuah, Jesus, our Lord. I pray for the peace of Jerusalem and protection for your people around the world. In the name of Jesus, Yeshua, by the power of the Holy Spirit, Amen.

Posted by lance at 4:44 AM

Tuesday, May 10, 2011

SCRIPTURE FOR TODAY PSALM 51:1-2

"Have mercy on me, O God, according to your unfailing love; according to your great compassion blot out my transgressions, wash away all my iniquity and cleanse me from my sin."

Posted by lance at 4:47 AM

PRAYER FOR TODAY

Father God Yahweh, Thank You for another day and a chance to do good and bring glory and honor to your name. Forgive me for my sins and help me to be strong in these last days. Bless me Lord with divine creativity and ideas to better my lot in this life. I ask for freedom from lack, joy, and happiness and a place in your kingdom. Bless me so I can be a blessing to others and share your word and resources with people I don't even know. Help me to understand your word and answer questions that people might have to get understanding and draw them closer to you. Lord, I pray for healing in my body and joy in my heart. I know I'm a sinful man and I need your mercy and grace for my salvation. Thank You Lord God. I pray for the peace of Jerusalem and protection for your people around the world. In the name of Yeshua, Jesus, Amen.

Posted by lance at 4:41 AM

Wednesday, May 11, 2011

SCRIPTURE FOR TODAY PSALM 40:1-3

"I waited patiently for the LORD; he turned to me and heard my cry; He lifted me out of the slimy pit, out of the mud and mire; he set my feet on a rock and gave me a firm place to stand. He put a new song in my mouth, a hymn of praise to our God. Many will see and fear and put their trust in the LORD."

Posted by lance at 4:51 AM

PRAYER FOR TODAY

Father God Yahweh, Help me to get through this day with joy despite the discomfort I feel. Help me to be in control of my mouth and think about what I say before I say it so as not to offend anybody or make myself seem foolish. Please help me to think of another way to make a living and provide for my family all their needs. You are my provider and I know you want only the best for me. Let me realize all the blessings you have in store for me beyond all that I could hope and ask for. I'm sorry for my sins, please forgive me and make me a better person. Thank You Lord God, in the name of Jesus, Yeshua, by the power of the Holy Spirit, I pray for the peace of Jerusalem and protection for your people around the world, Amen.

Posted by lance at 4:44 AM

Friday, May 13, 2011

SCRIPTURE FOR TODAY PSALM 54:1-4

"Save me, O God, by your name; vindicate me by your might. Hear my prayer, O God; listen to the words of my mouth. Strangers are attacking me; ruthless men seek my life--- men without regard for God. Surely God is my help; the Lord is the one who sustains me."

Posted by lance at 9:26 PM

Sunday, May 15, 2011

SCRIPTURE FOR TODAY PSALM 17:1-2

"Hear, O LORD, my righteous plea; listen to my cry. Give ear to my prayer--- it does not rise from deceitful lips. May my vindication come from you; may your eyes see what is right."

Posted by lance at 1:40 PM

PRAYER FOR TODAY

Lord God Yahweh, Please forgive me for my sins and where I fail to live a more righteous life. I know I am a sinful man and I need your mercy and grace for my salvation. Help me to renew my mind and change my way of thinking so I can experience all the blessings you have in store for me. Help me to bring glory and honor to your name in these last days so that more people might want to know you and seek you out and follow Yeshua, Jesus our savoir by the power of his blood. Help me to have self control and stop doing things I know to be wrong and that displease you. Thank you for always hearing my prayers and for your unconditional love and grace. In the name of Yeshua, Jesus our Lord and Savior I pray for the peace of Jerusalem and protection for your people around the world, Amen.

Posted by lance at 1:30 PM

Monday, May 16, 2011

SCRIPTURE FOR TODAY JOSHUA 1:8

"Do not let this Book of the Law depart from your mouth; meditate on it day and night, so that you may be careful to do everything written in it. Then you will be prosperous and successful."

Posted by lance at 4:42 AM

PRAYER FOR TODAY

Lord God, Yahweh, I don't understand myself, Lord. I keep doing the things I know aren't right and can't seem to get myself under control. I am sorry for my sins and I know I need You to help me to be a better person. Thank You for your word and all the wisdom and comfort it gives me, I'd be lost without it. Father, help me to find a better job, one that is cleaner and less hazardless and where there is more believers to help me. Help me to prosper and prepare for the coming hardships so I can be a blessing to my family and friends and bring glory and honor to your name. Thank you Lord, God, I praise your name, Yahweh, in the name of Yeshua, Jesus, our Lord and Savior, by the power of the Holy Spirit, Amen.

Posted by lance at 4:36 AM

Tuesday, May 17, 2011

SCRIPTURE FOR TODAY JOB 11:7-9

"Can you fathom the mysteries of God? Can you probe the limits of the Almighty? They are higher than the heavens---what can you do? They are deeper than the depths of the grave----what can you know? Their measure is longer than the earth and wider than the sea."

Posted by lance at 4:51 AM

PRAYER FOR TODAY

Father God, Yahweh, Lord Please help me to get out of the rat race I've been in all my life and help me to know true prosperity and freedom from lack. Show me the way to abundance and help me to do your will. I want to provide for my family all their needs and desires and give you the glory and honor. When someone says "how did you get that"? I will say, God gave it to me. I know you want your people to prosper and be in health according to your word. Let me experience all the blessings you can give. Joy unspeakable and peace in heart and mind. Help me to know these things. Thank You God, you are awesome, I love you and I love your ways and your Word. In the name of Yeshua, Jesus, the Messiah and our Lord and Savior, I pray for the peace of Jerusalem. Amen.

Posted by lance at 4:47 AM

Wednesday, May 18, 2011

SCRIPTURE FOR TODAY JOHN 14:1-

"Do not let your hearts be troubled. Trust in God; trust also in me. In my Father's house are many rooms; if it were not so I would have told you. I am going there to prepare a place for you."

Posted by lance at 4:42 AM

PRAYER FOR TODAY FOR THOSE WHO ARE IN FIRES AND FLOOD AND TORNADOS

Father God, Yahweh, Thank you for this day and all my blessings. Father I pray for those who are losing their homes and livelihood in fires and flood and tornados. Lord I ask that you comfort them and bless them with whatever they need to get back on their feet and prosper. I pray for those who have been killed and injured that comfort them and their loved ones and heal those that are injured and bring those that have died home to you. By the power of the Holy Spirit, in the name of Yeshua, Jesus, our Lord and Savior, Amen

Posted by lance at 4:36 AM

Thursday, May 19, 2011

SCRIPTURE FOR TODAY HEBREWS 11:1-2

"Now faith is being sure of what we hope for and certain of what we do not see. This is what the ancients were commended for. By faith we understand that the universe was formed at God's command, so that what is seen was not made out of what is visible."

Posted by lance at 4:48 AM

PRAYER FOR TODAY

Father God, Yahweh, thank you for all that you do for me every day, things I take for granted. Like having a place to live when many people are homeless, like having enough food to eat when many are hungry, like having decent clothes and clean water to drink and good health enough so I can work. Thank You Lord God for all of these and many other blessings to many to mention in this short prayer. How can I ask for more? I guess it's in my human nature to always want increase and to better my lot in this life. But I still give you thanks and glory for what I do have especially the knowledge and wisdom of your word and the hope of everlasting life with you in paradise with you. In the name of Jesus, Yeshua, our Lord and Savior I pray also for the peace of Jerusalem according to your word, Amen

Posted by lance at 4:37 AM

Friday, May 20, 2011

SCRIPTURE FOR TODAY 1 PETER 4:7-10

"The end of all things is near, therefore be clear minded and self-controlled so that you can pray. Above all love each other deeply, because love covers over a multitude of sins. Offer hospitality to one and other without grumbling. Each one should use whatever gift he has received to serve others, faithfully administering God's grace in its various forms."

Posted by lance at 4:34 AM

PRAYER FOR TODAY

Father God Yahweh, I thank You for being the great God that you are. The God of love and grace which is undeserved kindness. You tell the end from the beginning and warn us of what is coming upon this earth. Have mercy on me Father, I know I'm a sinner in need of a savior and I know You sent Jesus, Yeshua, Your son as a sacrifice for me and all those who believe your Word. Help me Lord to be a better person and to do your will as much as I can despite my sinful nature. I pray for peace of heart and mind, health, joy, happiness, safety, prosperity and a place in your kingdom for me and all my family. I also pray for the peace of Jerusalem according to your Word and protection for your people around the world. In the name of Yeshua , Jesus, our Savior, Amen.

Posted by lance at 4:24 AM

Saturday, May 21, 2011

SCRIPTURE FOR TODAY REVELATION 21:1-4

"Then I saw a new heaven and a new earth, for the first heaven and the first earth had passed away, and there was no longer any sea. I saw the Holy City, the new Jerusalem, coming down out of heaven from God, prepared as a bride beautifully dressed for her husband. And I heard a loud voice from the throne saying, "Now the dwelling of God is with men, and he will live with them. They will be His people, and God himself will be with them and be their God. He will wipe every tear from their eyes. There will be no more death or mourning or crying or pain, for the old order of things has passed away."

Posted by lance at 7:27 AM

PRAYER FOR TODAY

Father God Yahweh, Thank You for this beautiful day and all the blessings that go with it. Lord watch over my children and grandchildren and all my family and friends today and everyday as we move closer to the glorious coming of our Lord and Savior Jesus, Yeshua, Your Son and our King. Thank you for wisdom and knowledge and for the Holy Spirit that comforts and guides us in these last days. Help us to prepare for whatever trouble comes our way. "Let your kingdom come and your will be done on earth as it is in Heaven." According to your word, by the power of the Holy Spirit, and in the name of Jesus, Yeshua, I pray for peace in Jerusalem and forgiveness for my sins, Amen

Posted by lance at 7:14 AM

Sunday, May 22, 2011

SCRIPTURE FOR TODAY REVELATION 21:5-6

"He who was seated on the throne said, "I am making everything new!" Then he said, "Write this down, for these words are trustworthy and true." He said to me: "It is done. I am the Alpha and the Omega, the Beginning and the End. To him who is thirsty I will give to drink without cost from the spring of the water of life."

Posted by lance at 8:05 AM

PRAYER FOR TODAY

Heavenly Father Yahweh, I thank you Lord for being who you are, full of love and mercy and grace. For providing for us and caring for us and giving us your Word to guide us through this life you've given us. Help me to understand what it all means. Help me to do your will and share what wisdom and knowledge I receive from you and draw others closer to you by the power of the Holy Spirit. Help me to live a cleaner life and be a better model to those who don't know you yet. I'm sorry for my sins and ask you for forgiveness I thank You for all my blessings and ask that you watch over my family in these last days and keep us all safe and unharmed help us to prepare and be ready for the coming of our Lord Jesus, Yeshua the Messiah. I pray for the peace of Jerusalem and protection for your people around the world in the name of Jesus, Amen

Posted by lance at 7:56 AM

Monday, May 23, 2011

SCIPTURE FOR TODAY JAMES 3:13-

"Who is wise and understanding among you? Let him show it by his good life, by deeds done in the humility that comes from wisdom. But if you harbor bitter envy and selfish ambition in your hearts, do not boast about it or deny the truth. Such "wisdom" does not come down from heaven but is earthly, unspiritual, of the devil."

Posted by lance at 4:40 AM

PRAYER FOR TODAY

Father God Yahweh, Thank You Lord for your mercy and your undeserved kindness toward me. I know I'm a sinner and I need your forgiveness. I want you to wash me clean and cleanse me from all unrighteousness. Give me a better understanding of your word and the power of the Holy Spirit. Help me out of this rat race I'm in and let me know prosperity and abundance. Let me be an instrument of your divine creativity so I can better provide for my family. I worship you Lord God, Abba Father

Yahweh. I pray for peace in Jerusalem, protection for your people around the world. In the name of Jesus, Yeshua, Amen

Posted by lance at 4:32 AM

Tuesday, May 24, 2011

SPECIAL PRAYER FOR "LOUIS T." VICTIM OF STROKE

Father God I pray for the swift recovery of my attorney, Lou, Lord help him to get through this thing with no ill effects and be 100% whole and healthy. Let him continue to be a blessing to many as he helps those who make mistakes and who are in trouble. I ask also that you take away his desire for tobacco and cleanse his body from years of abuse. I ask also that you comfort his family and friends and let them know that you are in control and everything will be all right. In the name of Jesus, Yeshua, our Lord and Savior, make it so, Amen.

Posted by lance at 4:41 AM

SCRIPTURE FOR TODAY REVELATION 20:1-3

"And I saw an Angel coming down out of heaven, having the key to the abyss and holding in his hand a great chain. He seized the dragon, that ancient serpent, who is the Devil or Satan, and bound him for a thousand years. He threw him into the abyss and locked and sealed it over him, to keep him from deceiving the nations any more until the thousand years were ended. After that he must be set free for a short time."

Posted by lance at 4:31 AM

PRAYER FOR TODAY

Lord God, Yahweh, I thank You Father for another day of life and a chance to do good and bring glory and honor to your name and share your wisdom and word with others despite my sinful nature. My weakness is your strength. Lord god, help me to find a different way to provide for my family. Let me be an instrument of your divine creativity. Help me to prepare and be ready for the coming of Jesus, Yeshua, as I know it won't be long now and we will see him coming on a cloud, descending from heaven just as your word says. Come soon Lord Jesus! Set up your kingdom and rule for a thousand years according to your word. In the name of Jesus, Yeshua, our Lord, by the power of the Holy Spirit, Amen

Posted by lance at 4:22 AM

Wednesday, May 25, 2011

SCRIPTURE FOR TODAY REVELATION 22:1-2

"Then the angel showed me the river of the water of life, as clear as crystal, flowing from the throne of God and of the Lamb down the middle of the great street of the city. On each side of the river stood the tree of life, bearing twelve crops of fruit, yielding its fruit every month. And the leaves of the tree are for the healing of the nations."

Posted by lance at 4:44 AM

PRAYER FOR TODAY

Father God Yahweh, Thank you for your word to us. As I read it I am comforted to know that you have made provision for us to have a way better life in the future. Not what we experience in this life but eternal life in unspeakable joy and peace. Despite my sinful nature, you love me anyway and have made a way for me to be saved from everlasting destruction and a life without you. Help me to do your will and make you proud of me as I am of my own son. Thank you for your mercy and grace and unconditional love. In the name of Jesus, Yeshua, my Savior, I pray for the peace of Jerusalem and protection for your people around the world, Amen, make it so.

Posted by lance at 4:36 AM

Thursday, May 26, 2011

SCRIPTURE FOR TODAY PROVERBS 24:13-14

"Eat honey my son, for it is good; honey from the comb is sweet to your taste. Know also that wisdom is sweet to your soul; if you find it, there is a future hope for you, and your hope will not be cut off."

Posted by lance at 4:44 AM

PRAYER FOR TODAY

Father God Yahweh, Guide me Lord, by the power of the Holy Spirit, to a new way to make a living. I want change Abba Father. Help me to find a way to change my life for the better and be a great blessing to my family and friends and even people I don't know. Let me be an instrument of your divine creativity. Work in me Lord God so I can bring glory and honor to your name. Let me know freedom and peace and joy in this life and blessings beyond what I can ask or think. Lord I ask that you watch over all my family and friends in these last days and keep them safe. Lead us all on a path to your kingdom. I pray for the peace of Jerusalem by the power of the Holy Ghost and protection for your people around the world. And I ask for forgiveness for my sins in the name of Yeshua, Jesus, my Savior, Amen

Posted by lance at 4:38 AM

Friday, May 27, 2011

SCRIPTURE FOR TODAY PROVERBS 24:3-4

"By wisdom a house is built, and through understanding it is established; through knowledge its rooms are filled with rare and beautiful treasures."

Posted by lance at 4:40 AM

PRAYER FOR TODAY

Father God Yahweh, Help me to be a blessing to my family and friends and even people I don't know. Help me to strengthen my faith in you Lord. Help me to bring glory and honor to your name and do your will. Let your kingdom come and transform this world to paradise as you would have it. Father I pray also for the victims of the tornadoes in the south, comfort them and help them to recover from physical, emotional and financial setbacks and problems. Thank you for helping me cope with my own problems and for being there for me and for the forgiveness of my sins. I pray for the peace of Jerusalem and protection for your people around the world. By the power of the Holy Spirit, in the name of Yeshua, Jesus, my Savior, Amen.

Posted by lance at 4:36 AM

Saturday, May 28, 2011

SCRIPTURE FOR TODAY JOHN 1:1-4

"In the beginning was the Word, and the Word was with God, and the Word was God. He was with God in the beginning. Through him all things were made. In him was life, and that life was the light of men. The light shines in the darkness, but the darkness has not understood it."

Posted by lance at 7:19 AM

PRAYER FOR TODAY

Father God Yahweh, Thank you God for the Holy Spirit, that comforts us when things go wrong in our lives, and when we make mistakes. Help me to know the Holy Spirit better and know When He is speaking to me. Thank you God for all the good things in my life and thank You for forgiving me when I do wrong. Help me to turn away from wrong things and lead me to do good so I can feel good and have peace and joy in my heart. I love you God and I loves your ways and your Word. I pray for the peace of Jerusalem according to your word, by the power of the Holy Ghost, in the name of Yeshua, my Savior, Amen

Posted by lance at 7:12 AM

Sunday, May 29, 2011

SCRIPTURE FOR TODAY JOHN 1:14

"The Word became flesh and made his dwelling among us. We have seen his glory, the glory of the One and only, who came from the Father full of grace and truth."

Posted by lance at 1:10 PM

PRAYER FOR TODAY

Father God Yahweh, Thank you Lord for your grace that frees me from the penalty of sin. Thank you for forgiving me and loving me unconditionally. Let your kingdom come and your will be done on this earth as it is in heaven. You are the only true God and I'm glad you are the God I worship. Thank you for all my blessings and please watch over my children and grandchildren lead them to your kingdom. Help me be a great blessing to them and help provide for all their needs. I pray for the peace of Jerusalem and protection for your people around the world. In the name of Yeshua, Jesus, Amen.

Posted by lance at 1:06 PM

Monday, May 30, 2011

SCRIPTURE FOR TODAY JOHN 6:28-29

"Then they ask him, "What must we do to do the works God requires?" Jesus answered, "The work of God is this; to believe in the one he has sent.""

Posted by lance at 7:56 AM

Tuesday, May 31, 2011

SCRIPTURE FOR TODAY PSALM 88:1-3

"O LORD, the God who saves me, day and night I cry out before you. May my prayer come before you; turn your ear to my cry. For my sole is full of trouble and my life draws near the grave."

Posted by lance at 4:47 AM

PRAYER FOR TODAY

Father God Yahweh, Draw me closer to you Lord, I feel myself slipping away from you. Please don't let me get away from you. I do not want to go through the rest of my life without you. I'm sorry for my sins Lord I just cannot seem to control myself. Help me Lord God Abba Father. I want you in my life, to guide and direct me, to love me and protect me from all forms of accidents, disease and any enemies that might come against me. Help me to prosper in these last days so that I will be prepared and can help my friends and family when the time comes. I pray for strength and courage to do your will whatever you lead me to do. Watch over my children and grandchildren and keep them safe and unharmed and help me to be a blessing to them. And help me to bring glory and honor to your name. In the name of Yeshua, Jesus, my Savior, I pray for the peace of Jerusalem, according to your word. Amen.

Posted by lance at 4:41 AM

JUNE 2011

Wednesday, June 1, 2011

SCRIPTURE FOR TODAY PSALM 4:1

"Answer me when I call to you, O my righteous God. Give me relief from my distress; be merciful to me and hear my prayer."

Posted by lance at 4:33 AM

PRAYER FOR TODAY

Father God, Yahweh, Please help my children Lord, Help them to understand what's happening in the world today. Lessen the stress they feel and help them to have joy and peace and help them to prosper in these last days. Help us not to offend one and other and let there be no strife between us only love and compassion and understanding. Help me to be a great blessing to them as they are to me. I'm sorry for my sins and I ask for forgiveness in the name of Jesus, Yeshua, my Lord and Savior. I pray for the peace of Jerusalem, according to your word, By the power of the Holy Spirit, Amen

Posted by lance at 4:28 AM

Thursday, June 2, 2011

SCRIPTURE FOR TODAY 1 CORINTHIANS 10:23-26

"Everything is permissible"---but not everything is beneficial. "Everything is permissible" ---but not everything is constructive. Nobody should seek his own good, but the good of others.

Eat anything sold in the meat market without raising question of conscience, for, "The earth is the Lord's, and everything in it."

Posted by lance at 4:47 AM

PRAYER FOR TODAY

Heavenly Father, Yahweh, I need you Lord God, to Help me through the rest of my life. Give me courage and strength in these last days and help me to be a blessing to those I love. Let me be an instrument of your divine creativity and wisdom. Help me to share your word with others and draw them near to you by the power of the Holy Spirit. Let me know true peace, love, joy, and happiness in this life and a place in your Kingdom as it comes. Forgive me for my sins, I know I'm a sinful person and I need your mercy and grace for my salvation. Thank You Abba Father for sending Your Son Yeshua, Jesus, to die as a sacrifice for my sins and the sins of the world. I pray for the peace of Jerusalem, according to your word, In the name of Yeshua, Jesus, Amen

Posted by lance at 4:36 AM

Friday, June 3, 2011

SCRIPTURE FOR TODAY 2 CORINTHIANS 12:7-9

"To keep me from becoming conceited because of these surpassingly great revelations, there was given me a thorn in my flesh, a messenger of Satan, to torment me. Three times I pleaded with the Lord to take it away from me. But he said to me, "My grace is sufficient for you, for my power is made perfect in weakness." Therefore I will boast all the more gladly about my weaknesses, so that Christ's power will rest on me."

Posted by lance at 4:47 AM

PRAYER FOR TODAY

Father God, Yahweh, This is what I want; a place in your kingdom, peace of heart and mind, joy, love of family and friends, happiness, prosperity, abundance, and the health to enjoy it all. Help me to be a blessing to my children and grandchildren, Help me to provide good things for them and let us all live this life in peace and security and happiness. Help me with my self control issues, especially controlling my mouth. Forgive me for all my sins. Lord God, Abba Father, I pray for peace in Jerusalem and protection from all form of illness and accidents and the evil schemes of my enemies, according to your word, in the name of Jesus, Yeshua, Amen.

Posted by lance at 4:35 AM

Saturday, June 4, 2011

SCRIPTURE FOR TODAY EPHESIANS 1:3-5

"Praise be to the God and Father of our Lord Jesus Christ, who has blessed us in the heavenly realms with every spiritual blessing in Christ. For he chose us in him before the creation of the world to be holy and blameless in his sight."

Posted by lance at 4:44 AM

PRAYER FOR TODAY

Lord God, Yahweh, Thank You Father for all my blessings and help me to get better understanding of your word so I can share it with others according to your word. Let my faith be strong despite my sinful nature and weaknesses knowing that your power is made perfect in my weakness. Thank you for your word which comforts me in these last days and forgive me for all my sins. In the name of Jesus I pray for the peace of Jerusalem, Amen.

Posted by lance at 4:38 AM

Monday, June 6, 2011

SCRIPTURE FOR TODAY 2 THESSALONIANS 3:1-3

"Finally, brothers, pray for us that the message of the Lord may spread rapidly and be honored, just as it was with you. And pray that we may be delivered from wicked and evil men, for not everyone has faith. But the Lord is faithful, and he will strengthen and protect you from the evil one."

Posted by lance at 4:45 AM

PRAYER FOR TODAY

Lord God , Yahweh, Help me Lord, I just need your help in all areas of my life. Help me to be a better person and help me to bring honor to your name by the things I say and do. Let others know that the closer they get to you the better life can be. I only want joy and happiness in this life and a place in your kingdom in the next life. It would bring me great joy if only I could provide for all the needs and wants of my children and grandchildren. Bless me Lord so I can be a greater blessing. In the name Yeshua, Jesus, my Lord. Amen.

Posted by lance at 4:35 AM

Tuesday, June 7, 2011

PRAYER FOR TODAY

Lord God, Yahweh, Put my mind at ease and strengthen my faith, help me to know that you are my guide and my provider. Help me to share what I know and learn with others and bring honor to your name. I'm sorry for my sins and ask forgiveness. Let me receive all the fruits of the Holy Spirit and feel the joy that The Spirit gives. Let me be a blessing to my children and grandchildren and help them through these last days. I pray for peace in Jerusalem according to your word, in the name of Yeshua, Jesus, the Messiah and Savior, Amen

Posted by lance at 4:56 AM

SCRIPTURE FOR TODAY LUKE 12:22-25

"Then Jesus said to his disciples: "Therefore I tell you, do not worry about your life, what you will eat; or about your body, what you will wear. Life is more than food, and the body more than clothes. Consider the ravens: they do not sow or reap, they have no store room or barn; yet God feeds them. And how much more valuable you are than birds!" Who of you by worrying can add a single hour to his life?"

Posted by lance at 4:47 AM

Thursday, June 9, 2011

SCRIPTURE FOR TODAY MATTHEW 28:18-20

"Then Jesus came to them and said, "All authority in heaven and on earth has been given to me. Therefore go and make disciples of all nations, baptizing them in the name of the Father and of the Son and of the Holy Spirit, and teaching them to obey everything I have commanded you. And surely I am with you always, to the very end of the age".

Posted by lance at 4:54 AM

PRAYER FOR TODAY

Heavenly Father, Yahweh, Help me Lord to understand better why things are what they are. Thank you for your word that comforts me in these last days. Help me to help others and be a blessing to many in special ways. Let me be an instrument of your divine creativity. Let me be a great blessing to my family and supply all their needs and wants. Let me bring joy to their hearts. Help me to do your will in these last days and bring honor to your name. Forgive me for my sins and bless me so I can be a blessing. I pray for the peace of Jerusalem, according to your word, in the name of Yeshua, Jesus, the Savior, Amen.

Posted by lance at 4:47 AM

Friday, June 10, 2011

SCRIPTURE FOR TODAY JOHN 6:43-45

"Stop grumbling among yourselves," Jesus answered. "No one can come to me unless the Father unless the Father who sent me draws him, and I will raise him up at the last day. It is written in the prophets: "They will all be taught by God." Everyone who listens to the Father and learns from him comes to me."

Posted by lance at 4:50 AM

PRAYER FOR TODAY

Lord God, Yahweh, Help me to be a more giving person and a less selfish person. Help me to have more faith in you when it comes to doing something new as you do according to your word. Change me into a more effective follower of the Savior that I might bring glory to his name by showing others by example what he will do in their lives if they will only let him. Father, Abba, comfort those in grief today and make yourself known to the unbelievers that they might believe and have life and have it in abundance. Forgive me of my sin and watch over my children and grandchildren and keep them safe and unharmed in these last days and lead them on a path to your kingdom. I pray for the peace of Jerusalem, according to your word, in the name of Jesus, Yeshua, Amen,

Posted by lance at 4:38 AM

Saturday, June 11, 2011

SCRIPTURE FOR TODAY JOHN 7:16-18

"Jesus answered, "My teaching is not my own. It comes from him who sent me. If anyone chooses to do God's will, he will find out whether my teaching comes from God or whether I speak on my own. He who speaks on his own, does so to gain honor for himself, but he who works for the honor of the one who sent him is a man of truth; there is nothing false about him."

Posted by lance at 4:45 AM

PRAYER FOR TODAY

Father God, Yahweh, Thank you for all my blessings and for being a forgiving and loving Father, Thank you for making a way for me to have everlasting life. I believe that Jesus died for me as a sacrifice not only for my sins but for the sins of the whole world. All we have to do is repent and believe in the Lord Jesus, Yeshua our Savior. Help me to do your will which is to help others receive the free gift of everlasting life by words and deeds to bring glory and honor to your name and let as many as I can hear the "Good News" the Gospel message found in your word. Lord, please watch over my children and grandchildren and lead them on a path to your kingdom. I pray for peace in Jerusalem and protection for your people around the world, in the name Jesus, Yeshua, Our Messiah and Savior. Amen

Posted by lance at 4:37 AM

Monday, June 13, 2011

SCRIPTURE FOR TODAY JOHN 8:42-43

"Jesus said to them, " If God were your Father, you would love me, for I came from God and now I am here. I have not come on my own; but He sent me. Why is my language not clear to you? Because you are unable to hear what I say...."

Posted by lance at 8:53 AM

PRAYER FOR TODAY

Lord God, Yahweh, Thank You for another day and chance to serve you. Lord I pray for forgiveness for my sins and blessings for my children and grandchildren in these last days. Help me to be a blessing to all my family and friends. Help me with my self control problem, especially my mouth. Help me to think before I speak and to think about what I'm thinking about and replace wrong thoughts with good thoughts. Lord, help me to be an instrument of your divine creativity and work ideas that will be a blessing to many. Thank You for hearing my prayers. I pray for the peace of Jerusalem according to your word, in the name of Jesus, Yeshua my Lord and Savior, Amen.

Posted by lance at 8:47 AM

Tuesday, June 14, 2011

SCRIPTURE FOR TODAY JOHN 10:1-3

"I tell you the truth, the man who does not enter the sheep pen by the gate, but climbs in by some other way, is a thief and a robber. The man that enters by the gate is the shepherd of his sheep. The watchman opens the gate for him, and the sheep listen to his voice. He calls his own sheep by name and leads them out."

Posted by lance at 4:47 AM

PRAYER FOR TODAY

Father God, Yahweh, Thank you for wisdom and knowledge and the courage to use it to better my lot in life. I know it's your will that your people should have an abundant life and be free from lack and poverty. Bless me with peace, love and joy and all the fruits of your Holy Spirit that I would bring honor to your name. Help me to be a blessing to my friends and family. You are an awesome God the only true God and creator of heaven and earth and all that's in it. Thank you for being a God of love and grace and mercy. Thank You for Yeshua, Jesus our Redeemer and Savior and Messiah. I pray for peace in Jerusalem according to your word. In the name of Jesus, Yeshua. Amen.

Posted by lance at 4:40 AM

Wednesday, June 15, 2011

SCRIPTURE FOR TODAY JOHN 11:35

"Jesus wept."

Posted by lance at 4:54 AM

PRAYER FOR TODAY

Father God, Yahweh, These are the things I want; love, joy, peace, freedom from bad habits, prosperity, abundance, happiness, security, courage, strength, joy, peace, freedom, prosperity, divine creativity, love and respect from children and grandchildren, to do your will Lord, God. You are a good God and I'm happy that you are my God the one and only God. Thank You. Please bless me Father that I will be a blessing. Peace in Jerusalem and protection for your people around the world. According to your word, in the name of Jesus, Yeshua, Amen

Posted by lance at 4:51 AM

Thursday, June 16, 2011

SCRIPTURE FOR TODAY JOHN 14:23-24

"Jesus replied, "If anyone loves me, he will obey my teaching. My Father will love him and we will come to him and make our home with him. He who does not love me will not obey my teaching. These words you hear are not my own; they belong to the Father who sent me".

Posted by lance at 4:51 AM

PRAYER FOR TODAY

Father God, Yahweh, Help me to make wise decisions when I'm faced with them. Let me feel the Holy Spirit move in me and guide me to the best choices. Thank You for my good health and excellent prospects for my future and the future of my family. Let me be a blessing to all of them now and in the future. Thank you for setting me free to pursue other things of interest to me to better my lot in this life. Thank You for all my blessings. In the name of Jesus, Yeshua I pray for the peace of Jerusalem, by the power of the Holy Spirit, according to your Word, Amen.

Posted by lance at 4:45 AM

Friday, June 17, 2011

SCRIPTURE FOR TODAY ACTS 2:38-39

"Peter replied, "Repent and be baptized, every one of you in the name of Jesus Christ for the forgiveness of your sins. And you will receive the gift of the Holy Spirit. The promise is for you and your children and for all who are far off----for all whom the Lord our God will call.""

Posted by lance at 4:45 AM

PRAYER FOR TODAY

Father God, Yahweh. Thank You for all my blessings. Thank You for freedom and peace and joy unspeakable. Thank you for wisdom and knowledge and courage to try new things and discover new opportunities that will bless my family and me and even those that don't know me. Thank you for loving me enough to provide for me and supply all my needs according to your riches and glory. I will fear no evil thing because it is you who comfort me, according to your word. Thank you Lord God,

Abba Father, in the name of Yeshua, Jesus, by the power of the Holy Spirit, Amen.

Posted by lance at 4:38 AM

Saturday, June 18, 2011

SCRIPTURE FOR TODAY PSALM 122:6-9

"Pray for the peace of Jerusalem: "May those who love you be secure. May there be peace within your walls and security within your citadels." For the sake of my brothers and friends, I will say, "Peace be within you". For the sake of the house of the LORD our God, I will seek your prosperity.""

Posted by lance at 4:47 AM

PRAYER FOR TODAY

Lord God, Yahweh, Thank you for answering my prayers ! I can see everything coming together that I've been asking for. Thank You for all the fruits of the Holy Spirit, but I still need more help with self-control and will probably always need help in that area, but I know You are with me always according to your word and you are faithful to help us anytime. What an awesome God You are! The only true God. Lord, please continue to bless me and my family and let me be a blessing to many and bring honor to your name. Father, I pray for peace in Jerusalem and Israel according to your word, in the name of Yeshua, Jesus, my Savior, Amen.

Posted by lance at 4:37 AM

Sunday, June 19, 2011

SPECIAL PRAYER FOR PENNY WEST

Father God, Yahweh, Father we ask that you comfort your child Penny who is suffering from what may be cancer. I ask in the name of Jesus, Yeshua, our great Doctor that she be healed now, in this hour, of all that ails her. Help her to know that you are with her and that she has nothing to fear. Comfort her family and friends also and all those who are close to her. Glory and honor to your Holy name. Thank You Lord , in the name of Jesus, Amen

Posted by lance at 3:43 PM

SCRIPTURE FOR TODAY ECCLESIASTES 7:8-9

"The end of a matter is better than the beginning, and patience is better than pride. Do not be quickly provoked in your spirit, for anger resides in the lap of fools."

Posted by lance at 3:31 PM

PRAYER FOR TODAY

Father God, Yahweh, Thank you, Father for all my blessings. For my children and grandchildren and all my family and friends. Help me to be a blessing to all of them in these last days. Help me to prepare for whatever is coming our way and to have plenty to give and to share with any who may need our help. Bless me with divine creativity and give me ideas to use to better our lot in this life. Thank you for forgiving me of all my sins and short comings as I will also forgive all those who hurt me or seek to destroy me according to your word. Help me to be successful in whatever I put my mind to do. I pray for the peace of Jerusalem and protection for your people around the world. In the name of Yeshua, Jesus, my Lord and Savior. Amen

Posted by lance at 3:25 PM

Monday, June 20, 2011

SCRIPTURE FOR TODAY ECCLESIASTES 7:11-12

"Wisdom, like an inheritance, is a good thing and benefits those who see the sun. Wisdom is a shelter as money is a shelter, but the advantage of knowledge is this: that wisdom preserves the life of its possessor."

Posted by lance at 6:49 AM

PRAYER FOR TODAY

Lord God, Yahweh, Thank You Lord for always doing new things. And making all things new. Thank You for a new beginning. Give me confidence and courage as I start a new way to earn a living. Thank you for watching over me all these years as I was working in a dangerous occupation up until now. Thank you for my good health as I retire and start collecting my pension. Give me divine creativity and faith to make good things happen. I know you have a good plan for my life and I am waiting with keen expectation to see what good things you have in store for me. Please forgive me for my sins, I know I'm a sinful person and I need your mercy and grace for my salvation. I pray for the peace of Jerusalem and Israel in the name of Jesus, Yeshua, my Lord and Savior. Amen.

Posted by lance at 6:41 AM

Wednesday, June 22, 2011

SCRIPTURE FOR TODAY ECCLESIASTES 5:4-5

"When you make a vow to God, do not delay in fulfilling it. He has no pleasure in fools; fulfill your vow. It is better not to vow than to make a vow and not fulfill it."

Posted by lance at 6:44 AM

PRAYER FOR TODAY

Lord God, Yahweh, The earth is so beautiful and everything in it is amazing! I just wanted to let you know I appreciate the beauty you created for us, your children. Help me to be a better steward of this wonderful creation and guide me by the Spirit to do what You wish. I pray for forgiveness of my sins and I thank you for being a God of mercy and grace and generosity. Watch over all my family and friends and keep us all safe until your kingdom comes on this earth as it is in heaven. Help me to bring honor to your name some way every day. I pray for the peace of Jerusalem according to your word, by the power of the Holy Ghost and in the name of Yeshua, Jesus, our Savior and Messiah, Amen

Posted by lance at 6:33 AM

Friday, June 24, 2011

SCRIPTURE FOR TODAY ECCLESIASTES 5:2-3

"Do not be quick with your mouth; do not be hasty in your heart to utter anything before God. God is in heaven and you are on earth, so let your words be few. As a dream comes when there are many cares, so the speech of a fool when there are many words."

Posted by lance at 5:46 AM

PRAYER FOR TODAY

Heavenly Father, Yahweh, forgive me for my sins and weaknesses and help me to be stronger. Help me to resist temptation and control myself. I know that according to your word that your strength is made perfect in my weakness and that my sin is to let me be aware that I am in need of a Savior, Jesus, Yeshua my Lord. Thank you, God for making a way for me to see heaven and live forever in peace, love , joy, happiness and freedom. Thank you for watching over my children and grandchildren in these last days and help me to be a blessing to them. I pray for the peace of Jerusalem in the name of Jesus, Yeshua, the Messiah. Amen

Posted by lance at 5:38 AM

Sunday, June 26, 2011

SCRIPTURE FOR TODAY MATTHEW 24:36-39

"No one knows about that day or hour, not even the angels of heaven, nor the Son, but only the Father. As it was in the days of Noah, so it will be at the coming of the Son of Man. For in the days before the flood, people were eating and drinking, marrying and giving in marriage, up to the day Noah entered the ark; and they knew nothing about what would happen until the flood came and took them all away. That is how it will be at the coming of the Son of Man."

Posted by lance at 4:09 PM

PRAYER FOR TODAY

Lord God, Yahweh, Forgive me Lord for all my sins and selfishness. I want to be a better person. Help me to be the person you would want me to be. I want to be more generous, more caring , more loving , more understanding, more patient, more joyful, more peaceful and more wise. Thank you for knowledge and wisdom, help me to use these gifts to bring glory to your name and abundance in my life and the lives of my family. Thank you for a place in your kingdom despite my sinful nature. In the name of Jesus, Yeshua, my Lord and Savior, Amen.

Posted by lance at 3:45 PM

Wednesday, June 29, 2011

SCRIPTURE FOR TODAY ACTS 4:12

"Salvation is found in no one else, for there is no other name under heaven given to men by which we must be saved."

Posted by lance at 4:42 AM

PRAYER FOR TODAY

Lord God, Yahweh, Thank You for your mercy and your grace which is undeserved kindness and unconditional love. I know I'm a sinner in need of a Savior, Jesus, Yeshua, the only way to salvation and life everlasting. Please forgive me for my sins, I confess them all past present and future. Give me peace, joy, happiness, security, love, self control and prosperity me free from fear and anxiety. You are my God and there is no other, "greater is he that is in me than he that is in the world." Let me feel your presence and hear your voice, let me bring honor to your name by the things I do and say. Thank you for being my God. In the name of Yeshua,

Jesus, our Lord and Savior. I pray for peace in Jerusalem, according to your word, Amen.

Posted by lance at 4:39 AM

Thursday, June 30, 2011

SCRIPTURE FOR TODAY 2 TIMOTHY 1:6-8

"For this reason I remind you to fan into flame the gift of God, which is in you through the laying on of my hands. For God did not give us a spirit of timidity, but a spirit of power, of love and of self-discipline. So do not be ashamed to testify about our Lord, or ashamed of me his prisoner. But join with me in suffering for the gospel by the power of God,"

Posted by lance at 5:52 AM

PRAYER FOR TODAY

Father God, Yahweh, I decree a new and better life for my family and myself despite the way the world is today. With You in my life any good thing is possible and probable by the power of the Holy Spirit. Help me to bring honor to your name and make known to others that you are real and that your love is unconditional and never fails those who ask in the name that is above all others; Jesus, Yeshua our Savior and Messiah. I confess all my sins to you now Lord, past, present and future and I ask forgiveness in the name of Jesus, Yeshua and I also pray for the peace of Jerusalem, according to your word, by the power of the Holy Spirit. Amen.

Posted by lance at 5:43 AM

JULY 2011

Sunday, July 3, 2011

SCRIPTURE FOR TODAY PSALM 51:5-10

"Surely I was sinful at birth, sinful from the time my mother conceived me. Surely you desire truth in the inner parts; you teach me wisdom in the inmost place. Cleanse me with hyssop, and I will be clean; wash me, and I will be whiter than snow. Let me hear joy and gladness; let the bones you have crushed rejoice. Hide your face from my sins and blot out my iniquity. Create in me a pure heart, O God and renew a steadfast spirit within me."

Posted by lance at 6:34 AM

PRAYER FOR TODAY

Father God, Yahweh, Thank you Lord for being a God of mercy and grace. You are love and I know you love me unconditionally. That's why you sent Jesus, Yeshua here to be a sacrifice for the whole world to be saved. Thank you for giving me a chance to have everlasting life with you in heaven. I receive the free gift of eternal life in peace, joy and love with you in your kingdom and I will serve you all the days of my life. I pray you watch over my children and grandchildren and bless them with wisdom and knowledge and a place in your kingdom. Help me to be a blessing to them teach them the things I learn in the Spirit. Let them have the ears to hear and eyes to see. I pray for the peace of Jerusalem, according to your word, in the name of Jesus, Yeshua, Amen.

Posted by lance at 6:22 AM

Wednesday, July 6, 2011

SCRIPTURE FOR TODAY ISAIAH 61:10

"I delight greatly in the LORD; my soul rejoices in my God. For he has clothed me with garments of salvation and arrayed me in a robe of righteousness, as a bridegroom adorns his head like a priest, and as a bride adorns herself with her jewels."

Posted by lance at 1:26 PM

PRAYER FOR TODAY

Father God, Yahweh, Thank you Father for another day of your mercy and grace and forgiveness. Please help me everyday to be a better person to bring honor to your name and to live according to your word as best I can. I know I'm a sinful person and I need you in my life. Thank you for being a God of love and forgiveness. Bless my children and grandchildren with all the fruits of your Holy Spirit and a place in your kingdom. Bless me also Lord with freedom and prosperity, good health and a teaching spirit to share with others what I have learned from your Word. Peace in Jerusalem and protection for your people around the world. In the name of Yeshua, Jesus, according to your Word, Amen

Posted by lance at 1:14 PM

Thursday, July 7, 2011

SCRIPTURE FOR TODAY 1 PETER 2:1-3

"Therefore, rid yourselves of all malice and all deceit, hypocrisy, envy, and slander of every kind. Like newborn babies, crave spiritual milk, so that by it you may grow up in your salvation, now that you have tasted that the Lord is good."

Posted by lance at 3:56 PM

PRAYER FOR TODAY (DIVINE CREATIVITY)

Lord God, Yahweh, I ask for divine creativity to enable me to have a financial breakthrough. I can sense the urgency of the world situation and I feel the need to prepare for coming hard times. Lord, help me to be a blessing to my family and friends, that I will be in a position to help many overcome the hardships to come. I know I'm a sinful man but I still call You my Heavenly Father and my God. I thank you that your mercy and grace is new everyday and that Jesus paid the price for my sinful nature. Thank You for making a way for me when there seemed to be no way. According to your Word, by the power of the Holy Spirit, in the name of Jesus, make it so, Amen.

Posted by lance at 3:46 PM

Sunday, July 10, 2011

SCRIPTURE FOR TODAY 1 THESSALONIANS 5:16-18

"Be joyful always; pray continually; give thanks in all circumstances, for this is God's will for you in Christ Jesus."

Posted by lance at 10:08 AM

PRAYER FOR TODAY

Lord God, Yahweh, Thank You for all your teachers that teach and remind us of the power we have in you. That is prayer according to your Word and will. I thank you for truth and for your love and grace and mercy. Please help me to share what I learn according to your word that I can bring honor and glory to your name and your blessings on myself and my friends and family. Thank you for being my God and Father. I pray for the peace of Israel and protection for your people in the name of Yeshua, Jesus our Lord and Savior, Amen

Posted by lance at 10:03 AM

Monday, July 11, 2011

SCRIPTURE FOR TODAY 1THESSALONIANS 4:16-18

"For the Lord himself will come down from heaven, with a loud command, with the voice of the Archangel and with the trumpet call of God, and the dead in Christ will rise first. After that, we who are still alive and are left will be caught up together with them in the clouds to meet the Lord in the air. And so we will be with the Lord forever. Therefore, encourage each other with these words."

Posted by lance at 8:49 AM

PRAYER FOR TODAY

Heavenly Father, Yahweh, Thank You Lord for all my blessings. Help me to be a blessing to my children and grandchildren in these last days. Help me to prepare for the coming hard times and be ready to enter your Kingdom. Give me more of the Holy Spirit and let it be made manifest that people will see You working in me. I love you Lord God and I love your Word. Help me to understand it even better all the time. You are awesome God! Thank you for forgiving me for my sins and helping me to have joy in my life. I receive the free gift of everlasting life according to your Word in the name of Jesus, Yeshua, our Savior, and I pray for the peace of Jerusalem, Amen.

Posted by lance at 8:40 AM

Thursday, July 21, 2011

SCRIPTURE FOR TODAY ECCLESIASTES 3:1

There is a time for everything,
and a season for every activity under Heaven:

Posted by lance at 2:16 PM

GENERATIONAL CURSES??

Yes, I believe in generational curses because I was a part of one for a long time. I thank God it stopped with me and my children were spared the grief that goes along with this thing. Mine had to do with alcohol and depression, damaged relationships, broken homes, and lack, bad habits and selfishness. As far back as I can see my Dad and Grandpa on my Dads side and also the grandparents on my Moms side were all living with this kind of circumstance in their lives also. I am just recently coming out of this way of thinking which really is a curse and not that easy to break. But with Jesus, Yeshua, in Hebrew, it's not that hard. Knowing Jesus makes changing your way of thinking a lot easier. Reading my Bible also helps in changing destructive and unproductive thought patterns. I believe wrong thinking is a curse in its self because everything starts with a thought.

Posted by lance at 2:08 PM

Saturday, July 30, 2011

SCRIPTURE FOR TODAY PSALM 32:5

"Then I acknowledged my sin to You and did not cover up my iniquity. I said, "I will confess my transgressions to the LORD" - and You forgave the guilt of my sin."

Posted by lance at 2:36 PM

WHY I PRAY

I pray to God because I realize I cannot do everything by myself. I need a higher power than myself to help me. I choose to communicate with my creator because He is there to listen and to help me through the hard times we all go through.

The God I worship is the God of the Bible, not the Koran, not the book of Mormon, not any other 'holy book' but The Holy Bible. Inspired by the Creator of heaven and earth and all things there-in. Any other God is false and miss-leading.

I am a sinner by birth and will be a sinner till the day Jesus takes me home to be with Him in His kingdom. He paid the ultimate price for me and all of us to have everlasting life if we only receive the free gift of salvation that only He could render.

He has already answered so many of my prayers it's almost scary! He has protected me from harm, brought me thru certain addictions, blessed me financially, healed certain relationships and ended other relationships that were dangerous to me, He has just been there for me when I need Him. That's why I pray, because I know He is real and does reward those who diligently seek Him according to His Word. My God is awesome! He keeps strengthening my faith by working things out in my life. Some would call these things 'miracles' I just call them 'God Things' they happen so often

I have come to expect God to just be there anytime I need Him. I Thank Him continually and He keeps getting closer and closer to me. I praise His name in this little song He helped me write by the Holy Spirit:

THANK YOU LORD JESUS
Thank you Lord Jesus, for all my blessings;
Thank you Lord Jesus, for watching over me.
Thank you Holy Spirit, for all my wisdom,
Thank you Holy Spirit, for guiding me,

When the Holy Spirit shines His light on you,
There isn't no telling what the Lord can do,
He can heal the sick and make a blind man see-
Oh Lord, have mercy on me.
Thank You Lord Jesus, for all my blessings,
Thank you Holy Spirit for guiding me.

Your Word is revelation, for all creation.
Your Word is revelation, for us to see.
When the Holy Spirit shines His light on you-
There isn't no telling what the Lord can do.
He can heal the sick and make a blind man see,
Oh Lord, set the prisoners free.

I thank you Lord Jesus for all my blessings,
Thank You Lord Jesus for watching over me.
When the Holy Spirit shines his light on you,
There isn't no telling what the Lord can do.
He can heal the sick and make a blind man see-
He can lift a poor man out of poverty!

Thank You Lord Jesus, for all my blessings,
Thank you Lord Jesus, for watching over me.

Lance Freeze

Sing these lyrics or simply recite them like a poem every day for 30 days and you will see good things start to happen. There is no substitute for heart-felt prayer to your creator. All I know is that it has been working for me. Always remember this; Your Father in heaven loves you and wants the best for you. All he asks is that we receive what He gives us in faith believing that He is and that He does reward those who diligently seek Him and obey His word as best we can.

Posted by lance at 2:31 PM

Friday, August 5, 2011

ANSWERED PRAYERS

My most fervent prayers are being answered as I write this today!!! Praise the name of the Lord!!!! I praise You Yahweh ! I praise You Yeshua!! I praise You Holy Spirit!!!

Posted by lance at 2:38 PM

THOUGHT FOR TODAY

If you are a true believer, look to God for your blessings to come soon. If you are not a believer, look to man, (Elected Officials?) for your blessings to come, (when?)

Posted by lance at 2:34 PM

Sunday, August 7, 2011

BECAUSE I LOVE HIM

Because I love Him, today I will not lie to anyone, I will not steal from anyone; because of what He did for me, I will not be angry with anyone and I will forgive anyone who has done me wrong. Because He loves me, He has forgiven me for all my sin, past, present and future. Because He loves me He has given me the gift of life everlasting in the heavenly realm of reality. Because I love Him I will be a doer of His Word today. Because I love Him I will thank Him every day for all my blessings because HE IS REAL. L. Freeze

Posted by lance at 9:45 AM

SEPTEMBER 2011

Saturday, September 3, 2011

ZECHARIAH CHAPTER 9

Read this in your own bible, it tells us what will shortly take place in Israel. Read the whole book of the Prophet Zechariah it will enlighten you on why things are the way they are. Who's side would you rather be on? I myself am on the side of God's chosen people anything else is sheer stupidity. Who else has the Word of eternal life? Surely not Islam. They teach we get to heaven by our good works. In that case none of us would make it. Jesus taught we get to Heaven by Gods grace and His shed blood as a sacrifice for the sins of the whole world. Salvation comes as a free gift of God. Grace through faith so that no man can boast is the only way. We need only to trust Jesus and receive our gift and do our best to be obedient to His Word. God is good all the time!!! Accept Him as your Lord and Savior today!!! Just say this-- Lord Jesus, I believe you died for me and you were resurrected and are now sitting at the right hand of the Father in heaven. Please come into my heart and be my Lord and Savior. Thank You LORD! In the name of Jesus, Yeshua The Messiah, Amen

Posted by lance at 9:15 AM

SUPPORT ISRAEL

We as believers need to support Israel because they are Gods chosen and who ever Blesses them will be blessed by Yahweh just as His word says. Islam is a false religion that wants to war against anyone who disagrees with their way of life which is death. We as Christians are grafted in with the Jewish people and are spiritual Israelites so we will share in the inheritance that God provides for His People. He will destroy whoever comes against His people, including the united nations, even the U.S. if we don't stand up for Israel and support them when all their enemies attack them, which will be sooner than later because of all the changes going on in the middle east. All the countries against Israel will soon try to destroy her and that will start world war 3. Get ready people! get right with God and pray for Israel , bless them with financial support, moral support, stand up for them in these last days and The God of Heaven will bless you just as His word says.

Posted by lance at 8:55 AM

Sunday, September 18, 2011

PEACE OF JERUSALEM

Pray for the peace of Jerusalem because radical Islam wants to take over and annihilate Israel and eventually impose 'Sharia' law on the entire planet. This week is going to be very interesting if the U.N. allows the Palestinians to be a member state. Israel will simply not stand for it. If they insist on the '67' borders for a two state solution there will be war on a large scale in the mid-east. It's all prophesied in the bible. God will protect His people. The radical Muslims will learn then who the true God really is. So I urge everyone to pray for Israel and Jerusalem, get on the side of the true God, Yahweh and the Messiah Yeshua, He has plans for those of us who are faithful. Plans to prosper us and keep us and deliver us in the times of trial and hardship. He will bless those who bless Israel and curse those who curse Israel. It is written in His word and His Word is true.

Posted by lance at 5:56 PM

OCTOBER 2011

Sunday, October 16, 2011

SCRIPTURE FOR TODAY MATTHEW 8:13

"It shall be done for you as you have believed."

Posted by lance at 5:49 PM

PRAYER FOR TODAY

Lord God I thank You for this day and all my blessings. For my Children and grandchildren, for all my family and friends, for wisdom and knowledge, for health and well-being, and for answering my prayers. You are and awesome God and creator, the only God because there is no other. Thank You for drawing me closer to You. Father, I pray and ask for Your continued blessings and that Your Holy Spirit continue to guide and direct me according to Your Word. That I am a blessing to my family and others that may not even know me. Help me to be a doer of Your Word and strengthen my faith and increase my wisdom and knowledge that I may share these things with others to be a blessing and to bring glory and honor to Your name. In the name of Jesus, Yeshua, our messiah I pray for the peace of Jerusalem, peace for Israel and protection for Your people around the world, make it so.

Posted by lance at 5:41 PM

NOVEMBER 2011

Tuesday, November 1, 2011

ABOUT ISLAM

What I know about Islam is that the Muslim extremists have control over the 'peaceful' Muslims by fear and intimidation. They seek to control the world by whatever means necessary. They are a hateful religion and believe that to die for 'Allah' is the ultimate way to use their lives. They hate anyone who isn't a Muslim and consider that person an infidel. Those who refuse to convert to Islam will be killed by the sword or gun. They treat women as slaves and condone beatings and disfigurement for disobedience. The Koran was written by the profit Muhammad way after Christianity was established.

The feud between Muslims and Jews goes way back to the time of Abraham. Ishmael was the father of the Arab nations and Isaac was the father of the Jewish nation. God blessed the Jews as His chosen people and the Arabs also were blessed but not as God's chosen. They were blessed with great wealth, 'oil'. In the end, Gods chosen people will prevail over their enemies. Arabs want war, Jews want peace. Arabs want to take the land that God promised Israel, be it such a small sliver of land compared to the vast land God blessed the Arabs with. War is inevitable in the near future. Look at the signs in the Arab world and the growing anti-Semitism. Keep in mind God says in the bible that He 'will bless those who bless His people, and will curse those who curse Israel'. He will protect His own. Blessed be Israel!! Glory to the God of Abraham, Isaac and Jacob!!! Pray for the peace of Jerusalem! Come quickly Lord Jesus! 'Let Your will be done in earth as it is in heaven' AMEN!

Posted by lance at 4:41 PM

Thursday, November 3, 2011

DAILY PRAYER

Lord God, I just thank you for all my blessings and for answering my prayers. I know You are real and I am thankful that You have called me to be closer to You. You give me wisdom and knowledge through your Word and You comfort me and guide me with Your Holy Spirit. I thank You. Help me to be a better person and a blessing to my family and even others that don't know me to bring glory and honor to Your name not mine. Protect us , Father from all forms of sickness, disease, accidents, and attacks by the enemy. Peace for Jerusalem and protection for Your people around the world. In the name of Yeshua, Jesus, our Messiah, make it so.

Posted by lance at 10:08 AM

DECEMBER 2011

Tuesday, December 27, 2011

THE PREISTLYBLESSING NUMBERS 6:24-26

"The LORD bless you and keep you; the LORD make His face shine upon you and be gracious to you;

The LORD turn His face toward you and give you peace."

This is a very powerful scripture. I believe we will be blessed if we pass this on to other believers. Join me in blessing others that may not know this.

Posted by lance at 4:36 PM

Saturday, December 31, 2011

HAVE A BLESSED AND PROSPEROUS 2012

May the joy, peace, and love of God be with you always. Be blessed in all that you do! Amen

Posted by lance at 1:23 PM

COME INTO AGREEMENT WITH SOMEONE FOR ANSWERED PRAYER

That's what the WORD says, that we can agree on certain things with each other in prayer and it will be done for us if we do it according to the WORD. So right now this minute, who ever reads this post will be blessed with this blessing-- Numbers 6:24-26 "The LORD bless you and keep you; the LORD make His face shine upon you and be gracious to you; the LORD turn His face toward you and give you peace."

" Blessed are You LORD our God, King of the universe who instructs us in His ways". Give us peace, freedom, joy, health, prosperity, abundance and protection from all forms of accidents, illness, sickness, disease and attacks by the enemy. Bless us LORD to be a blessing. In the name of Jesus, Yeshua, our Messiah, make it so.

Posted by lance at 1:20 PM

FEEL LED

I just feel led to share this scripture with everyone again because I believe it is a very powerful scripture when said out loud or written down. I need all the blessings I can get from God and don't mind sharing that . I believe if we bless each other with this God given scripture we can call down the awesome blessings of God for each other. The Word says that if two or more believers come into agreement for anything in the name of "Jesus" it will be done for them. I want to be blessed with peace of mind, freedom, love, joy, health, prosperity and abundance. "Blessed to be a blessing" to others, to bring glory and honor to God and to enjoy all the blessings that the Father has in store for me, His child. Do you want the same things? If you do, then let's agree together and ask God in prayer in the name of JESUS. Let me know if you agree.

Posted by lance at 1:03 PM

THE BLESSING GOD GAVE MOSES TO AARON TO THE PEOPLE

"The LORD bless you and keep you;

the LORD make His face shine upon you and be gracious to you;

the LORD turn His face toward you and give you peace." Numbers 6:24-26

Posted by lance at 12:49 PM

JANUARY 2012

Sunday, January 1, 2012

ANOTHER YEAR CLOSER

Well, we are another year closer to our destiny, which is to usher in the Kingdom of God on earth. I realize we have a few more things to go thru before we can see Him coming on the clouds to take charge of the world. Israel will be attacked soon and a major war will erupt in the mid-east, we all know this. I believe that will begin the events that will lead up to Jesus return. "Come quickly Lord Jesus". Yeshua, our Messiah!

Posted by lance at 8:06 AM

Monday, January 2, 2012

ANSWER ME THIS

Why in the worldl do people who profess to be intelligent insist on believing in evolution??!! It does not make sense. Don't they know that the energy that made them happen is still working in all of us today? Design requires a designer, who designed your eye??? Who put that on paper? Why? Who prompted you to speak? Why do we want to create something? Why is there 'choices' ? Why 'right' or 'wrong'? Why is there 'good' and 'evil'? It can only mean that 'God' is real and that we all should be aware that the enemy, Satan is trying to mislead us in what we tend to think. It's all in our thoughts, our minds are the grounds of our salvation.

Posted by lance at 11:18 PM

BLESS YOU ! NUMBERS 6:24-26

"THE LORD BLESS YOU AND KEEP YOU; THE LORD MAKE HIS FACE SHINE UPON YOU AND BE GRACIOUS TO YOU; THE LORD TURN HIS FACE TOWARD YOU AND GIVE YOU PEACE."

Posted by lance at 10:50 PM

Tuesday, January 3, 2012

PROVERBS 15:16

"Better a little with the fear of the LORD than great wealth with turmoil."

Posted by lance at 9:51 AM

Wednesday, January 4, 2012

PRAYER

LORD God, Thank You for Your Word and the wisdom that always comes with it. I pray for Your favor to be with me and that I understand the wisdom of Your Word that I will share it with others as the Spirit prompts me. Protect us from all forms of accidents and illnesses, sickness and disease and all attacks from the enemy. Help us to know the blessings you have in store for us and let us know joy, peace, love, freedom from lack, prosperity, health, divine creativity and abundance. In the name of Jesus, Yeshua our Messiah, make it so.

Posted by lance at 9:19 AM

JAMES 4:7-8

Submit yourselves, then, to God. Resist the devil, and he will flee from you. Come near to God and He will come near to you. Wash your hands, you sinners, and purify your hearts, you double-minded."

Posted by lance at 9:06 AM

Thursday, January 5, 2012

WHAT'S UP WITH IRAN?

What's up with Iran threatening us? Don't they know we are still the greatest power on earth? Do they have some kind of secret weapon or something? They seem to want trouble. They evidently do not value human life.

We who worship the God of Abraham, Isaac, and Jacob. The creator of heaven and earth, the Great "I am that I am, Yahweh or Jehovah, our God, we value life and liberty. They who worship Allah, seem to value death and murder and hatred. Who will prevail in the upcoming war? The Koran doesn't tell us anything about it. Our Bible tells us everything in detail. Guess what? We win! Praise God almighty!

GOD BLESS ISRAEL!! GOD BLESS THE U.S.A.!!

Lets all pray for Israel and the peace of Jerusalem. God says, "I will bless those who bless you and I will curse those who curse you".. I don't know about you, but I for one want all of God's blessings. I want all of His promises. I want His Kingdom to come and His will to be done on earth as it is in Heaven. In the name of Jesus, Yeshua, Our Messiah, Make it so.

Posted by lance at 3:12 PM

JAMES 4:13-15

"Now listen, you who say, "Today or tomorrow will go to this or that city, spend a year there, carry on business and make money." Why, you do not even know what will happen tomorrow. What is your life? You are a mist that appears for a little while then vanishes."

Posted by lance at 2:47 PM

Tuesday, January 10, 2012

SOMETHING TO THINK ABOUT

When we pray do we call down things from heaven that we don't want? How do we talk to our God? How about just making decrees and declarations of the things we want to manifest in our lives not the things that may dominate our thought lives. Let the things we ask God for be on our minds not the things we don't want. We should not let negativity dominate our thoughts, "I can't..., they won't..., no one will..., no one does...., I'm not strong enough to...., and so on. God gave us all a certain amount of faith and power, it's up to us to learn how to use it. SPEAK blessings into your life by using positive words. Say out loud in the morning, "I am blessed and start saying what you want not what you don't want.

Posted by lance at 9:16 AM

ROMANS 10:9-10

"That if you confess with your mouth, "Jesus is Lord", and believe in your heart that God raised Him from the dead, you will be saved. For it is with your heart that you believe and are justified, and it is with your mouth that you confess and are saved."

Posted by lance at 8:58 AM

DECREE AND DECLARE

"I am blessed in the city and blessed in the country. My children are blessed and the work of my hands is blessed. I am blessed when I come in and blessed when I go out." Taken from Gods Word in Deuteronomy the 28th chapter. These are some of the blessings for obedience. I declare and decree these in my life. I declare and decree prosperity, divine health, unspeakable joy, abundance, freedom, peace, love, and divine creativity. Thank You LORD God!! In the name of JESUS, YESHUA our Messiah

Posted by lance at 8:46 AM

Saturday, January 14, 2012

POWERFUL WORDS

I did not realize how powerful our words really are until I saw Cindy Trimm on "Its Supernatural" with Sid Roth. Wow, it does make perfect sense because God created everything with just a "Word". And if we are created in the image of God then we should have a certain amount of power inherited from our "Father" in heaven. The knowledge of this power is the first step to changing our circumstances in many ways.

Lets say we have a desire for something, we then ask God for whatever it is and we don't see anything manifest as soon as we would like so we give up. The Word says, "keep asking, keep knocking, keep seeking". O.K. Let's try this again, a different way, lets verbalize our request. For example, "I decree and declare abundance and prosperity in my life. I declare that I am a blessing to my family and friends. I am a blessing to people that I don't even know. I give generously and God gives back to me generously. I am free to travel. I have no fear. I am an instrument of divine creativity. I give thanks to God daily."

When we ask, let's ask for the 'means' to get what we want not the specific thing. Let's ask for 'wisdom' instead of money or stuff. Then all the things we want will come to us if it is in God's will. If things we want are not in line with the will of God then O. K. So I ask for, wisdom, peace, freedom, prosperity, abundance, joy, health, love, blessings to be a blessing, to bring glory and honor to God. Speak these kind of things out loud everyday and watch what happens. Wisdom to you. These things are the will of God and our power to call down blessing from heaven. Peace to you.

Posted by lance at 9:19 AM

THE LAW OF EXPECTATION

"And we can be confident that He will listen to us whenever we ask Him for anything in line with His will. And if we know He is listening when we make our request, we can be sure that He will give us what we ask for." 1 John 5:14-15

Posted by lance at 8:45 AM

Sunday, January 15, 2012

PASS THIS ON

"THE LORD BLESS YOU AND KEEP YOU;
THE LORD MAKE HIS FACE SHINE ON YOU
AND BE GRACIOUS TO YOU;
THE LORD TURN HIS FACE TOWARD YOU
AND GIVE YOU PEACE". Numbers 6:24-26

This is the blessing God gave Moses to bless Gods people. These are powerful words for the ones who put their faith in the Living God. Pass this on to someone you love and keep these words in your heart and you will be blessed. Watch things begin to change in a most blessed way. In the name of Yeshua, Jesus, our Savior, make it so.

Posted by lance at 9:30 AM

Monday, January 16, 2012

PRAYER

Lord God thank You for all my blessings. According to Your Word we are suppose to ' keep on asking, keep on knocking and keep on seeking, and You will give us what we are wanting. Father, I want peace, freedom, joy, love, health, prosperity, abundance, divine creativity, and to be a blessing to my family and friends. Father thank you for blessing me with all good things, things that are in line with Your will and Word. Thank You in the name of Yeshua, Jesus, by the power of the Holy Spirit and according to Your Word I pray for the peace of Jerusalem. Make it so.

Posted by lance at 4:19 PM

PSALM 24:1-2

"The earth is the LORD'S, and everything in it, the world, and all who live in it; for He founded it upon the seas and established it upon the waters."

Posted by lance at 4:05 PM

Tuesday, January 17, 2012

PSALM 122:6

"Pray for the peace of Jerusalem: May they prosper who love you...."

Posted by lance at 10:15 AM

IS 2012 REALLY "IT"?

Well, all the signs point to this being the last year of life as we know it. SIGN 1: Israel restored Jerusalem back to the Jews. Israel rebirth in one day in 1948. The desert will bloom and blossom. In her short existence, Israel became the largest exporter of roses to Europe. The Hebrew language has been brought back to life.(Zephaniah 3:9 NKJV) SIGN 2: Israel surrounded by conflict and the rise of global anti-Semitism. SIGN 3: The regathering of the Jewish people physically back to the land of Israel from the 4 corners of the earth. SIGN 4: The Gospel is proclaimed to the nations. SIGN 5: The blindness coming of the eyes of the Jewish people. (Romans 11: 25) SIGN 6: Fullness coming to the church. Look again at

Posted by lance at 9:30 AM

Wednesday, January 18, 2012

SCRIPTURE FOR TODAY

"If you remain in me and my words remain in you, ask whatever you wish, and it will be given you. This is to my Father's glory, that you bear much fruit, showing yourselves to be my disciples." John 15:7-8 WOW!!!

Posted by lance at 1:43 PM

TRY JUST ASKING....

In the Gospel of John Jesus was comforting His disciples by explaining to them all they had to do for His help was simply ask. Look at John 14:12-14 it says: "I tell you the truth, anyone who has faith in me will do what I have been doing. He will do even greater things than these, because I am going to the Father. And I will do whatever you ask in My name, so that the Son may bring glory to the Father. You may ask me for anything in my name and I will do it." Jesus can't be any clearer than this. He repeated Himself to make sure they "got it". I have been asking out loud lately when I used to just ask in my silent prayers. That seems to reinforce my confidence or something I don't know but I do know that God has been answering my prayers. Sometimes He takes longer than I want to wait but He answers them just the same. All we have to do is, by faith, follow the instructions. Try it!! Just ask and keep asking till He makes it happen!

Posted by lance at 1:17 PM

Saturday, January 21, 2012

1 TIMOTHY 1:15-16

Paul writes: "Here is a trustworthy saying that deserves full acceptance: Christ Jesus came into the world to save sinners-- of whom I am the worst. But for that very reason I was shown mercy so that in me, the worst of sinners, Christ Jesus might display His unlimited patience as an example for those who would believe on Him and receive eternal life."

Posted by lance at 9:21 AM

THANK GOD FOR...

I thank God for His grace, which is undeserved kindness and favor. I thank Him for His patience with me as I learn His ways through His Word and His servants. I thank Him for giving His one and only Son as a ransom sacrifice for the sins of the world past, present, and future. Embrace HIM! In the name of Jesus, Yeshua, our Savior and Lord, Amen

Posted by lance at 9:11 AM

Sunday, January 22, 2012

ROB GOD?

Malachi Chapter 3:8-12 Says: "Will a man rob God? Yet you rob me.

"But you ask, 'How do we rob you'?

"In tithes and offerings. You are under a curse---the whole nation of you---because you are robbing me. Bring the whole tithe into the storehouse, that there may be food in my house.

Test Me in this, says the LORD Almighty, "and see if I will not throw open the floodgates of heaven and pour out so much blessing that you will not have room enough for it. I will prevent pests from devouring your crops, and the vines in your fields will not cast their fruit," says the LORD Almighty. "Then all the nations will call you blessed, for yours will be a delightful land," says the LORD Almighty."

Posted by lance at 9:56 AM

Monday, January 23, 2012

DONT BE AFRAID?

Fear not, that's what Jesus said many times to His disciples. I believe He was trying to tell them a secret that He wants all of us to know.

Those of us who are saved can rest assured that God is watching over us. He is protecting us and guiding us by the power of the Holy Spirit. The problem is, that even as "believers" we have a hard time really believing it until we actually see a sign or have some sort of experience.

I have had many good things happen in my life since I began "asking" "seeking" "knocking" and following the lead from the Holy Spirit. It seems like one minute, I'm one way, and then, I'm different somehow, I think I could call it a "transformation". It's that I have changed my way of thinking about my situation.

When you just "let go and let God" then things get easier to change. You start to make certain decisions more wisely. You find yourself in different places and around different people.

It's so cool how God works! "I aint scared." Don't you be either.

"The LORD bless you and keep you;

The LORD make His face to shine upon you and be gracious to you;

The LORD turn His face toward you and give you peace." Numbers 6:24-26

Posted by lance at 10:38 AM

Tuesday, January 24, 2012

HEIRS?

If we believe, then we are in line for an inheritance. According to Paul as he writes to the Galatians; "If you belong to Christ, then you are Abraham's seed, and heirs according to the promise". Galatians 3:29

Wow, can you imagine the blessing that would be! The promise here is salvation from everlasting destruction to everlasting life in His kingdom. Not to mention the power we get from the Holy Spirit.

When we receive Jesus as our Lord and Savior, we also get the "fruits of the Spirit"; Love, Joy, peace, kindness, mildness, faithfulness, patience, self-control, and goodness. With all those come more blessings when we exhibit them to the world. With all those virtues bubbling out of us we are the envy of the world.

Thank You Lord God, for all these blessings. Help me to be a blessing in these last days. Help me to do Your will and serve You and be a light to the lost. Let me hear Your voice and feel Your touch on my life. Help me to share all the knowledge and wisdom You give me with others so that they might receive You as their Lord and Savior. Father, bless me with abundance in every good thing so that I might share with those in need and bring glory and honor to Your name. Let Your kingdom come and Your will be done on earth as it is in Heaven. Protect us from all forms of accidents, illness, sickness, and attacks from the enemy. In the name of Yeshua, Jesus, our Savior and Messiah, make it so.

Posted by lance at 8:28 AM

Wednesday, January 25, 2012

PAUL SAYS....

"For I am convinced that neither angels nor demons, neither the present or the future, nor any powers, neither height nor depth, nor anything else in all creation, will be able to separate us from the love of God that is in Christ Jesus our Lord." Romans 8:38-39

This is really good news! Count on it!

Posted by lance at 8:52 AM

Thursday, January 26, 2012

WHAT DO YOU THINK?

"Finally, brothers, whatever is true, whatever is noble, whatever is right, whatever is pure, whatever is lovely, whatever is admirable--- if anything is excellent or praiseworthy---think about such things." Philippians 4:8

This is a very powerful scripture! This is ancient wisdom, the stuff they don't teach in schools! No one taught me that if I train my thoughts and think about peace, and beauty, and happiness and plenty, all these things would come to me without effort. So, instead I let my thoughts be polluted with what the schools wanted me to think about and the T.V. and radio, movies, newspapers and so on. I was at the mercy of my own performance in the world. I did not perform well. That's why I lived in lack, fear, uncertainty, and just a general feeling of anxiety. This Word of God is life changing to the believer. Get as much of the "WORD" in you as possible and let it transform you from the inside out!

Posted by lance at 9:40 AM

YOU'RE HERE!!

It's no mistake you've found this site today. If you are not "Saved" you can be saved right now. Just say this out loud: "Jesus, I believe in you. I believe you gave your life to save me and I believe you rose again and sit at the right hand of the Father. I confess all my sin and I ask forgiveness. I ask You Jesus to come into my heart and I receive You as my Lord and Savior. Thank You LORD! I am saved!

Now, according to the Word of God, you are saved and are an heir to a promise made by our Creator made possible by Jesus, Yeshua our Messiah. His shed blood paid the price for not only your sin, past, present and future, but the sin of the whole world. All those who receive Jesus Christ are brought under the wing of Almighty God and are given special gifts. I encourage you to read about these "gifts" for yourself in God's Word. Start with the Gospel of John. May God bless you with wisdom and understanding in Jesus name, Amen

Posted by lance at 9:17 AM

Friday, January 27, 2012

GIVE THANKS?

"Give thanks to the LORD, for He is good; His love endures forever." Psalm 107:1

Posted by lance at 5:13 PM

HEY ISLAM!

LIFE IS BETTER THAN DEATH,LOVE IS BETTER THAN HATE, FREEDOM IS BETTER THAN BONDAGE, TRUTH IS BETTER THAN LIES, Muslims die for Allah, Christ died to give us life, "For God so loved the world that He gave His one and only Son, that 'WHOEVER' believes in Him shall not perish but have eternal 'LIFE.' For God did not send His Son into the world to condemn the world, but to save the world through Him". John 3:16

THIS MEANS YOU!! RECEIVE IT!

Posted by lance at 8:53 AM

Sunday, January 29, 2012

"NO EYE HAS SEEN"?

"No eye has seen, no ear has heard,
no mind has conceived what God has prepared
for those who love Him". 1Corinthians 2:9

Wow! Can you imagine?

Posted by lance at 5:37 PM

BE JOYFUL ALWAYS?

"Be joyful always; pray continually; give thanks in all circumstances, for this is God's will for you in Christ Jesus." 1 Thessalonians 5: 16-18

There has got to be a reason why God would want us to be so contrary to our 'nature'. When we make the effort to 'do this "word" and not just hear it then the blessings and answered prayers will come. It works for me. It will for you too. Lord God, I ask for love, joy, peace, freedom, prosperity and abundance make themselves real in the lives of all those who read this prayer and say it. I ask for divine creativity, divine health and security, confidence, boldness and increase in faith. Let all these things manifest in the lives of those who believe. Thank You Lord God, in the name of Jesus, Yeshua our Messiah and Savior, Make it so.

Posted by lance at 11:45 AM

ANSWERED PRAYERS?

I found out that when I pray for someone else the same things I want for myself, (Health, peace, freedom, joy, love, abundance, prosperity), the sooner these things become real in my life. I can honestly say that God has answered my prayers for these kind of things. Look, what else is there?

Don't ask God for material things! "Seek first the Kingdom and all these other things will be added to you"... There is no such thing as "lack" in the Kingdom of God. There is no such thing as hate, sickness, war, bondage, misery, and poverty in the Kingdom of God. So when we pray let's ask for the things of the Kingdom. God will bless us and then we can be a blessing to someone else. That's what it's all about brothers and sisters! Jesus said, "Pray for those who curse you and mistreat you....." in the Sermon on The Mount. (The Gospel of Luke Chapter 6.) Now why would He want us to pray for our enemies and those who don't like us? It' because when we pray for others we will receive God's blessings in our own lives. It may not make sense to us but it's true just the same.

Posted by lance at 11:23 AM

Monday, January 30, 2012

DESPITE YOUR SINFUL NATURE....

Listen, despite our sinful nature, Jesus died for us anyway. Do not let that hold you back from drawing closer to God. In fact, we sinners have the advantage, why? Because 'Jesus came to seek and to save' people like us!! When we take a step toward Him He will take two steps toward us!

I don't care how much you smoke, drink, do drugs, or watch porn. When you get more of the 'Word' in you than those sinful things the bad will purge out of you and will gradually, just go away. Satan is a liar! He puts all these stumbling blocks under our feet in hopes that we will be drawn away from God. And it works a lot of the time. We can still overcome all these things that we 'think' will send us to hell or keep us separated from God's love. JESUS WANTS YOU! Despite your sinful nature. He will change you. Effortlessly. If we only keep coming to Him in prayer and ask Him to forgive us, read His word, listen to His servants who preach and teach His Word. May God richly bless you, starting NOW!

Posted by lance at 2:31 PM

WHAT JOHN SAID.....

"I write these things to you who believe in the name of the Son of God so that you may know that you have eternal life.

This is the confidence we have in approaching God: that if we ask anything according to His will, He hears us. And if we know that He hears us---whatever we ask---we know that we have what we have asked of Him." 1 John 5:13-15

Posted by lance at 8:53 AM

Tuesday, January 31, 2012

BE STILL?

"He makes wars cease to the ends of the earth;

He breaks the bow and shatters the spear,

He burns the shields with fire.

'Be still, and know that I am God;

I will be exalted among the nations, I will be exalted in the earth." Psalm 46: 9-10

Posted by lance at 1:43 PM

JEWISH ROOTS?

How often do you think about the Jewishness of Christianity? Jesus was a Jewish Rabbi and His given name is Yeshua the Hebrew form of Jesus. Many Jewish people are being led to Him in these last days as the day approaches when He will return on the clouds and begin His Kingdom on earth.

Almost all of the old testament prophesies about Him have been fulfilled and the Gospel or 'good news' about Him and what He has done for mankind is being preached in all the inhabited earth for a witness to His glory, to the 'Jew first' then to the gentiles or non-Jew. These Jews who have put their faith in Yeshua as Messiah are known as Messianic Jews. They are on the increase even in Israel. They did not stop being Jewish because they now believe in Jesus and Jesus did not stop being Jewish because He is the Messiah.

So, I feel the need to explore the Jewish roots of Christianity. So far I find it very revealing because I've been exposed to ancient Jewish wisdom. I find myself wanting to celebrate the Jewish holidays instead of the Christian holidays because these are the days That God said were to be celebrated. Christmas and Easter were decreed sacred by men 325 years after Jesus. So what is more important to you? What God says? Or what men say?

Posted by lance at 1:24 PM